Social Media Ethics and COVID-19

Social Media Ethics and COVID-19

Well-Being, Truth, Misinformation, and Authenticity

Edited by
Pamela A. Zeiser and Berrin A. Beasley

LEXINGTON BOOKS
Lanham • Boulder • New York • London

Published by Lexington Books
An imprint of The Rowman & Littlefield Publishing Group, Inc.
4501 Forbes Boulevard, Suite 200, Lanham, Maryland 20706
www.rowman.com

86-90 Paul Street, London EC2A 4NE

Copyright © 2023 by The Rowman & Littlefield Publishing Group, Inc.

All rights reserved. No part of this book may be reproduced in any form or by any electronic or mechanical means, including information storage and retrieval systems, without written permission from the publisher, except by a reviewer who may quote passages in a review.

British Library Cataloguing in Publication Information Available

Library of Congress Cataloging-in-Publication Data

Names: Zeiser, Pamela, editor. | Beasley, Berrin, 1970- editor.
Title: Social media ethics and COVID-19 : well-being, truth, misinformation, and authenticity / edited by Pamela A. Zeiser and Berrin A. Beasley.
Description: Lanham : Lexington Books, [2023] | Includes bibliographical references and index.
Subjects: LCSH: Social media—Moral and ethical aspects—United States. | Misinformation—United States. | COVID-19 Pandemic, 2020—United States.
Classification: LCC HM741 .S6335 2023 (print) | LCC HM741 (ebook) | DDC 175—dc23/eng/20220922
LC record available at https://lccn.loc.gov/2022037243
LC ebook record available at https://lccn.loc.gov/2022037244

ISBN: 978-1-66691-186-2 (cloth)
ISBN: 978-1-66691-188-6 (pbk.)
ISBN: 978-1-66691-187-9 (ebook)

Contents

Introduction　　1
Berrin A. Beasley and Pamela A. Zeiser

PART I: SOCIAL MEDIA, COVID-19, AND TRUTH　　7

1. Attempting to Stop the Spread: Epistemic Responsibility
   and Platformed Responses to the COVID-19 "Infodemic"　　9
   Miles C. Coleman

2. Hashtag Populism: Plandemics, Scamdemics, and Viral Resistance　　31
   Linda Howell

3. Social Media, COVID-19, Misinformation, and Ethics:
   A Descriptive Study of American Adults' Perceptions　　53
   Tammy Swenson-Lepper and Heidi J. Hanson

PART II: SOCIAL MEDIA, COVID-19, AND WELL-BEING　　83

4. Exploring the Impact of COVID-19 on Leisure through
   Social Media　　85
   Annette M. Holba

5. COVID-19 at the Nexus of Social Media and Propaganda:
   Public Health Messaging on Twitter amid Political Polarization　　109
   Berrin A. Beasley and Pamela A. Zeiser

6. Divisiveness, Meaningful Lives, and the Hope of Compassion:
   Social Media in the Time of COVID-19　　125
   Mitchell R. Haney

Appendix: Chapter 3 Survey Instrument	149
Index	157
About the Contributors	161

Introduction

Berrin A. Beasley and Pamela A. Zeiser

Because it can be used for both good and ill, social media poses ethical challenges for corporate providers, government officials, and users. Misinformation and disinformation abound for every topic posted to platforms, and social media lacks the ethical gatekeepers of traditional media. Few firm answers have been found to questions about these challenges, including the following: What responsibility do corporate providers bear for inaccurate information posted by users? What responsibility do users bear? In this "post-truth" and polarized world, who defines "accurate information"?

These vexing questions of social media and ethics existed well before the global outbreak of the coronavirus pandemic in March 2020. Yet some of the best and worst moments of this significant global event would result from the nexus of social media and ethics. As a way for users to both produce and consume information, social media is a tool that could be used for considerable good in the COVID-19 pandemic—public health agencies were already using social media to disseminate information and trace contacts. Emergency management agencies and traditional news media already used social media to track information during disasters. Individual users could find communities for shared values or experiences, such as illness, quarantine loneliness, maintaining social connections, and filling leisure time during the lockdown. All of these existing advantages to social media could contribute to the international, national, local, and individual responses to the COVID-19 pandemic. At the same time, however, the disadvantages were obvious as well; users—including government officials—could post and amplify inaccurate or misleading scientific and health information; engage in discrimination and hate against scapegoated minorities, especially those of Asian heritage; and escalate conspiracy theories detrimental to public health. Such drawbacks of social media have proven detrimental to the response to COVID-19.

This edited collection is intentionally multidisciplinary in investigating the multifaceted relationship between social media and COVID-19; it brings together work from scholars in the disciplines of communication, English, philosophy, and political science. In doing so, it provides different disciplinary perspectives on the ethical use of social media (or the lack thereof) during the COVID-19 pandemic—perspectives which can be supplementary and complementary. For example, while only Beasley and Zeiser (from the disciplines of communication and political science) look directly at tweets by government officials and agencies, contributors Haney (philosophy), Howell (English), Swenson-Lepper and Hanson (communication) all address the ethicality or impact of former president Donald J. Trump's dissemination of misinformation via Twitter. Together, these disciplines and chapters reinforce each other; some information found within them is new and different, complementing each other, while other information is similar and supplements its validity when found by scholars in different disciplines.

Why use a multidisciplinary approach? Because a broader array of disciplinary perspectives on the ethical use of social media during COVID-19 can lead to a broader understanding of the use of social media for COVID-19, and potentially a broader array of tools to manage the challenges found at the nexus of social media, ethics, and COVID-19. For example, Coleman (communication) analyzes the tools established by social media platforms to prevent COVID-19 misinformation and disinformation, while Haney (philosophy) presents tools for prompting individuals who have accepted disinformation to rethink or question their opinions. Information and analyses from multiple disciplines give us a better chance to solve or manage real-world challenges than information and analysis from just one discipline (Klein and Newell 1997, 394). The ethics of social media will remain such a real-world challenge in and of itself, for COVID-19, and for future global crises.

This book is divided into two sections. The first section deals with social media and the value of truth. Authors in this section address the top-down versus bottom-up techniques social media platforms use to regulate misinformation, the copiability of messaging containing disinformation and the communal ownership of narratives, and American perceptions of ethical and truthful use of social media during the pandemic. The second section explores social media and well-being. Here, the authors consider the positive role of social media for our increased leisure time and social distance during the pandemic, reactions to the use of social media for public health messaging and the communal good, and the positive and negative roles of social media for meaningful lives during COVID-19. In this way, the contributors to this volume answer the earlier questions of corporate responsibility, user responsibility, and responsibility for accurate information through four main topics: misinformation, truth, well-being, and authenticity.

In the first chapter, Miles C. Coleman analyzes how social media platforms attempt to deal with misinformation to ensure truth and accuracy that contribute to user well-being. This includes the automated tools they use to decide whether to flag misinformation, attach corrective statements or links to it, or delete the content entirely. Specifically, he considers whether Reddit, YouTube, and Twitter are transparent in their creation and application of misinformation-prevention policies and the direction by which such policies are formed and implemented—top-down or bottom-up. Coleman's analysis shows that each platform has policies that are mixtures of fully transparent or fully bottom-up. Those mixtures have benefits and disadvantages for all actors involved; Coleman finds ongoing ethical tensions between freedom of speech, profit-making by the social media companies, and user well-being during the pandemic.

Linda Howell's emphasis on misinformation, truth, and well-being in chapter 2 offers a sobering and nuanced analysis of the communal ownership and copiability of conspiracy theories on social media. Focusing specifically on the scamdemic and plandemic hashtags on Twitter, she examines frequently the retweeted tweets for rhetorical devices or patterns of diction that indicate engagement. Within the larger frame of suspicion of the government, media, and major corporations, she finds three themes emerging from #scamdemic and #plandemic tweets and retweets: technodemia, parental rights, and medical cynicism. Howell concludes that the "COVID-19 misinformation loop" is both dangerous to individual users and grounded in how groups use social media to form communities and make meaning.

Chapter 3, by Tammy Swenson-Lepper and Heidi J. Hanson, is different from and complementary to other chapters, which primarily focus on social media platforms and individuals as their users. Instead, Swenson-Lepper and Hanson provide valuable context based upon a public opinion survey about how respondents felt or now feel about ethical issues when they themselves or family and friends used social media during the COVID-19 pandemic. At the time this book was conceived, no research had been done measuring people's feelings about ethical issues surrounding their or their family members' use of social media during the pandemic, which was a key missing piece of the investigation into social media use during COVID-19. Their chapter engages with misinformation, truth, well-being, and perceptions of individual authenticity. Swenson-Lepper's and Hanson's results show that political polarization via social media is a concern for survey respondents, which resonates with themes in Beasley and Zeiser, Haney, and Howell. The same concern exists for civil rights, tolerance, and communal responsibility during the pandemic. Swenson-Lepper's and Hanson's findings, tied to the theory of Third-Person Effect, demonstrate the concern respondents have for family and friends when the platform guidelines discussed by Coleman fail.

Those very same respondents could benefit from Haney's analysis of how misinformation and disinformation impact individuals—as well as his model of compassionate listening to perhaps change the beliefs of those accepting questionable information.

In chapter 4, Annette M. Holba presents perhaps the most positive discussion of the use of social media during COVID-19 as she evaluates its contributions to meaningful leisure as a factor of well-being. Holba acknowledges that social media has caused damage during the pandemic but focuses on its advantages. Particularly during lockdowns but also self-isolation, social media usage expanded across all age groups as people sought to creatively adapt and find ways to retain human connections as well as fill their leisure time. Holba emphasizes the ways in which social media allows for "useless" occupation, which allows individuals to focus on meaning-making in leisure. One example is online tourism. She also emphasizes the debate over structured versus unstructured leisure time and the ways in which social media contributed to both during the pandemic. The study of leisure considers its impact on the human condition, just as Holba considers the impact of social media during COVID-19 on leisure.

In chapter 5, Berrin A. Beasley and Pamela A. Zeiser examine whether Twitter users responded to tweets by the White House, the U.S. Centers for Disease Control, and a journalist as propaganda or persuasion. Utilizing Jowell and O'Donnell's (2019) three categories of persuasion response—shaping, reinforcing, and changing—they analyze public health posts regarding mask-wearing and replies to them on Twitter. Their findings reveal that what some users see as useful information prompting necessary changes for the good of the community, other users see as discrimination, oppression, or based upon ulterior motives. Beasley and Zeiser propose that individuals, for their own well-being and for societal well-being, have a responsibility to critically analyze social media messaging for misinformation, and they propose that individuals utilize Jowett and O'Donnell's (2019) definitions of persuasion and propaganda to evaluate social media messages as either truthful or deceptive.

In chapter 6, Mitchell R. Haney starts by asking how one should approach family or friends seeking to be their authentic selves in ways that are surprising departures from their own past or societal norms. Within the context of political polarization and the COVID-19 pandemic, Haney hypothesizes about how society and individuals respond to the moral challenges of individual freedom versus the public good. How do individuals come to accept questionable social media narratives about the pandemic? What roles do platform's guidelines and profit-making play in that process? Given the concepts of European liberalism, success, and moral luck, what can individuals do when family or friends base their authentic selves on social media narratives built on misinformation or disinformation? Compassionate listening—a method for asking questions, finding common ground, and prompting self-reflection—is one tool society and individuals can use to overcome polarization and the impact of narratives of disinformation on social media.

This edited volume is an exploration of how the advantages and disadvantages of social media complicated the COVID-19 pandemic. Multiple disciplinary perspectives are employed to study social media as a complex and rapidly evolving form of communication. In particular, the ethical challenges of social media include questions of misinformation, truth, well-being, and authenticity. We hope that by focusing on these topics we may contribute to the understanding of the ethical (or lack thereof) use of social media during the COVID-19 pandemic.

REFERENCES

Jowett, Garth S., and Victoria O'Donnell. 2019. *Propaganda and Persuasion*. 7th ed. Thousand Oaks, CA: SAGE.

Klein, Julie T., and William Newell. 1997. "Advancing Interdisciplinary Studies." In *Handbook of the Undergraduate Curriculum: A Comprehensive Guide to Purposes, Structures, Practices, and Change*, edited by Jerry Gaff and James Ratcliff, 393–415. San Francisco, CA: Jossey-Bass.

Part I

SOCIAL MEDIA, COVID-19, AND TRUTH

Chapter 1

Attempting to Stop the Spread

Epistemic Responsibility and Platformed Responses to the COVID-19 "Infodemic"

Miles C. Coleman

With respect to productive public deliberation, the social web is equal parts good, bad, and ugly. We can share and connect with others at the click of a button. But, for the same reason, the social web also poses the threat of garbage information and cockamamie behavior. In this chapter, I retrace some of the nuanced tensions between freedom of speech and the responsibilities of social media platforms to counter the badness (i.e., misinformation) and ugliness (i.e., aggression) of the social web with rules, guidelines, and practices that uphold the good (i.e., the ability to productively engage in *knowing well*).

After establishing a definition of epistemic responsibility within the context of misinformation on social media as well as the competing demands for expediency and dialogue that characterize moments of public crisis, I will discuss the pragmatic and ethical trade-offs involved in different "platformed" approaches to misinformation on the social web during the COVID-19 pandemic. Namely, I will describe two basic term sets useful for identifying, defining, and drawing out the ethical and pragmatic trade-offs of varying approaches. The first term set is that of *closed/open*, designating consideration of *how* the rules and processes of enforcing those rules are, or are not, visible to community members. Some platforms *close* off their rules and processes, while others brandish them *openly*. The second term set is *top-down/bottom-up*, which deals with *where* the rules about misinformation come from. Some platforms invite *bottom-up* definition of the rules, handing it over to the community on a given platform to define and enforce, whereas other platforms may take a more *top-down* approach where the rules are defined by platform administrators. Each of these approaches intersect in unique matrices, bringing with them ethical and pragmatic trade-offs, which

I track into current practice by analyzing the approaches of three major social media platforms: Reddit, YouTube, and Twitter.

THE PROBLEM OF "INFODEMICS" AND EPISTEMIC RESPONSIBILITY: KNOWING WELL AND CONNECTING WELL

February 2020, at the outset of the COVID-19 pandemic, Tedros Adhanom Ghebreyesus, director of the World Health Organization, explained that "we're not just fighting an epidemic; we're fighting an *infodemic*" (as cited in World Health Organization 2020; emphasis added). An *infodemic* names the phenomenon of the overwhelming amount of information in response to public crises, which involves both reliable and unreliable sources competing for attention and trust, creating a situation amid the pandemic wherein discerning the right thing to do was made difficult. Placed at the center of the infodemic, alongside other outlets of information, was social media (World Health Organization 2020). The ease with which persons can access and share information outside of the traditional "checks" for accuracy and reliability (such as what one might find in a traditional newspaper, for instance) means that social media platforms lend themselves not only to speedy sharing of information, but also accidentally inaccurate *mis*information, or even worse, purposely misleading *dis*information.

The COVID-19 infodemic highlighted a unique ethical problem for social media platforms regarding the responsibility of persons to be informed community members, or what Lorraine Code (2020) names *epistemic responsibility*. Epistemic responsibility, as Code articulates it, is the upholding of *intellectual virtue*: the quality of character that we associate with the activity of *knowing well*. Knowing well is an activity characterized by the responsibility to seek out information, especially concerning matters that can impact the community. "I didn't know," in other words, is not enough, for one also has a responsibility to know. To fall down in this duty is to fail in upholding epistemic responsibility, to lack intellectual virtue as someone who should be actively working to know well. In some ways, social media offers a means of exercising intellectual virtue. But, during an infodemic, even if persons do seek out information in efforts to know well, the sheer abundance of information, including misinformation and disinformation, creates a moment in which persons might be acting in the spirit of intellectual virtue, but in ways that nonetheless fail to uphold the good of the community. Amid an infodemic, there exists the very real complication of epistemic responsibility, changing things from a matter of "I didn't know" to "I don't know what to believe." Consequently, for social media platforms such as Reddit, YouTube, and Twitter, a further layer of epistemic responsibility manifests not merely as the activity of knowing well, but, further, as the activity of cultivating spaces in which knowing well can take place. As Code (2020) puts it, "human beings are essentially social and leads one to see that knowledge acquisition, as an activity of such beings, is a communal activity. Intellectual virtue manifests itself in communities that impose constraints and conditions upon *acceptable knowledge seeking* at the same time as they make that activity possible" (253; emphasis added). The responsibility of social media platforms amid the COVID-19 infodemic, moreover, involves facilitating the activity of knowledge seeking (e.g., in allowing for open discussion and information sharing) while also imposing constraints on what counts as acceptable knowledge seeking (e.g., in enforcing the sharing of scientifically accurate information)—to create spaces in which knowing well can take place.

An important factor entangled with the cultivation of spaces on the social web where knowing well can take place is the phenomenon of online aggression, or the use of tactics such as doxxing, flaming, or hate-speech tactics used by the intolerant to silence the tolerant (Reyman and Sparby 2019). It is difficult to know well when reasonable persons are silenced by persons who do not argue with reasons but rather with threats or attacks. The responsibility for platforms in pursuing the facilitation of knowing well, put differently, is not merely a matter of triaging and flagging misinformation, but also of including and enforcing ground rules of interaction that protect community members from such silencing aggressions, for knowing well relies upon *connecting well*. As *custodians of the internet*—Tarleton Gillespie's (2018) guiding metaphor regarding the responsibility of platforms—despite the general appeal of platforms being "hands-off" on defining rules of communication, or the idea that it is the responsibility of users to be "civil," social media platforms have a duty to *define* and *enforce* rules of interaction in response to the needs of the community (Reyman and Sparby 2019). Knowing well is a communal activity, and as such, it is dependent on *connecting well*.

In response to misinformation, the actions of social media platforms, as we will see below, vary, originating from different sets of assumptions about the best approach to cultivating spaces for connecting and knowing well amid the COVID-19 pandemic. And, further complicating matters is that, for better or worse, private companies have a major role to play in public health crises that simultaneously (and seemingly paradoxically) demand expediency *and* dialogue.

THE DEMAND FOR EXPEDIENCY (AND DIALOGUE) AMID THE COVID-19 INFODEMIC

Some claims are indeed a waste of time. "The COVID vaccine will turn you into a monkey," for instance, is a claim that is radically out of touch with scientific fact and does not serve the public with the ability to make informed decisions. To give such a claim any attention, especially during an infodemic where even the scientifically accurate information is overwhelming in its volume, would seem only to make matters worse. And, so, in the spirit of expedient action, a platform might unilaterally remove such a claim from its feeds. But a funny thing happens when information (even throw-away, waste-of-time information) is *removed* from view: It introduces the possibility that *something is being hidden*. Such an action might strike some at an ethical level as performed by a platform that does not recognize a need to be answerable to public. At worst, it might further fuel conspiratorial discourses by affording members of pseudoscientific publics an inventional resource that can be leveraged to reify the misinformed claim by representing "truth" beyond hidden agendas (see Coleman and Cypher 2020; Coleman 2017): "See! They removed the post, proving that there is a mass coverup of the monkeyizing effects of the vaccine!"

The cultivation of spaces of knowing well is further complicated by the fact that social media platforms, while serving public discussion, are nonetheless owned and operated by the *private* sector. As Amitai Etzioni (2019) explained just months before the pandemic about *fake news*, or journalistic articles that perpetuate misinformed facts:

> Removing fake news may seem at first a rather straightforward task. For instance, it's a no-brainer to delete reports that Hillary Clinton ran a sex ring out of a Washington, D.C., pizzeria. But in many cases the line between fake news and the rest is blurry. Many news stories that grossly mislead and manipulate have a small kernel of truth, but its significance is vastly overstated and misinterpreted. (22)

In Etzioni's view, misinformation such as fake news can have deleterious effects on a community. That community's ability to know well is impacted. But, at the same time, imposing constraints on communication should not be a matter handled behind closed doors, out of view of the general public. Rather, "the best that can be done is to insist that the source be disclosed. Then the public can decide which sources to trust" (Etzioni 2019, 22). Etzioni's advice draws out an important tension inherent to the work of dealing with misinformation in ways that cultivate spaces for knowing well. Namely, in a pragmatic sense, while acceptable knowledge seeking on social media platforms seems to require expediency in the form of private companies imposing constraints, those constraints cannot be defined in isolation from the broader user community without dialogue.

Social media companies employ various strategies, including, but not limited to, flagging misleading claims, attaching corrective statements, or removing content altogether. Many of these strategies are implemented with the help of automation, which further exacerbates a sense of *black-boxing* of decision-making, in that the process of enforcing control over information flow is harbored within the backend of proprietary systems, ostensibly minimizing accountability (Perel and Elkin-Koren 2017). Such models of moderating public discussion, for some, are attended by worries (like Etzioni's above) that public discussion is being shaped by private companies, serving their own agendas, independent of community concern. Put in ethical terms, seeming efforts to protect human flourishing by controlling misinformation, finds itself in tension with utilitarian appeals to freedom of speech, entangled with the material realities of for-profit companies' making decisions *for* publics rather than the other way around.

By contrast, there are also approaches, wherein, rather than identify and act upon misinformation solely with opaque processes from the "back end," the community writ large is invited to identify and comment on possible misinformation. Such "open-source" approaches to flagging and addressing misinformation seem to be novel ways to engage the ethical tensions inherent to more black-boxed approaches. Of course, the approach is also characterized by rhetorical problems, having to do with the perceived credibility of users who post flags and commentary (Pröllochs 2021), which tracks further with other research that shows that corrections of misinformation amid emerging social issues are effective when originating from a source with an established reputation, such as the U.S. Centers for Disease Control and Prevention, or that corrections by unknown users are more effective when accompanied by credible links while noting that corrections from unknown users might also risk *backfire effects* (Vraga and Bode 2017; Nyhan and Reifler 2010). The point being that the best route to platformed interventions into misinformation on social media is not straightforward, for even interventions that are moored in the broader dialogue of a user community can carry direct implications to the ability of a community to know well.

The sheer volume of information about the COVID-19 pandemic requires expediency on the part of platforms to help persons quickly "sift" through the deluge of information and to pick out the best information. Reversing the *pollution* of the infosphere, in other words, is one way this intuition has been articulated and is in line with the general assumption that controlling the flow of information is probably the most effective strategy available to avoid misinformed publics (Cotter, DeCook, and Kanthawala 2022). But the infodemic also requires dialogue, rendered in the form of answerability between platforms and the publics they serve. The tricky thing here is that both expediency and dialogue are valuable, especially during a public health crisis. Resultantly, some platforms prioritize expediency and others dialogue, resulting in different "procedural" (Bogost 2007; Brock and Shepherd

2016) performances of epistemic responsibility. In the following section, I describe an array of procedural responses to the demands of the COVID-19 infodemic, using two term sets, both dealing with different aspects of expediency and dialogue. The first term set is open/closed, having to do with *transparency* of decision-making. And, the second term set is top-down/bottom-up, having to do with the *directionality* of defining the rules of a platform (e.g., whether rules and processes are defined by the community or the platform or both).

NAVIGATING THE COMPETING NEEDS FOR EXPEDIENCY AND DIALOGUE: THE MATRIX OF TRANSPARENCY AND DIRECTIONALITY IN PLATFORMED RESPONSES TO MISINFORMATION

Amid a public health crisis, like the COVID-19 pandemic, it seems that the quicker the better in regard to getting important information to persons as they make decisions that can affect individual and public health. However, competing with the need for speed is the need for trust in the information in the first place, something facilitated by open dialogue among persons as they weigh options, interrogate ideas, and measure evidence to arrive at conclusions. Where some may have categorical commitments to dialogue (this author certainly does), it is also true that to engage in dialogue is to slow down the process of arriving at a conclusion—something that seems at odds with being able to act quickly, especially when it means quibbling with someone that thinks a COVID-19 vaccine will turn them into a monkey. Where some people may have patience for dialogue with persons who are misinformed on science, others might see that patience as affording unearned legitimacy to the misinformed by seemingly entertaining the idea that they, in fact, have *something* to discuss (Ceccarelli 2011; Coleman 2018b). These competing intuitions about the right thing to do in communication with the misinformed translate into the context of platformed responses to misinformation. Some platforms demonstrate proclivities toward dialogue, and others, expediency, performed in various approaches to openness (or closedness) of the processes of censure as well as whether the rules of censure are "handed down" by the platform administrators or "handed up" by the user community. Before exploring the various permutations of these approaches in the "wild," I will first offer more definition of open/closed and top-down/bottom-up approaches, while underscoring some of the ethical and pragmatic trade-offs of each, starting first with transparency of process in the term set open/closed, and then moving to the directionality of rule-making and enforcement in the term set top-down/bottom-up.

Transparency: Open and Closed Approaches

When thought of in general terms, it is nearly a truism that *transparency* is better than opacity when it comes to public discussion and decision-making on the social web. This is especially so amid such phenomena as platform-derived censorship, which can serve "commercial logics and interactions with the state, rather than the protection of civil rights and a democratic public sphere" (Hintz 2015, 122). Put differently, private companies can control public discussion from the backend, hidden from public scrutiny, shaping public discussion unbeknownst to the common user (Hintz 2015). Having the conversation that Platform-X *wants* us to have is not the same as having the conversation that we *need* to have. Being able to check *digital repression* requires access to the processes that a company employs, or not, to sculpt public discussion on its feeds (Kendall-Taylor, Frantz, and Wright 2020), including not just what the rules are, but how those rules are applied to make decisions in specific cases (Suzor, West, Quodling, and York 2019). Given that many applications of censure occur through automation, and are "black-boxed," a problematic lack of accountability emerges on the part of the platform, resulting in an imbalance of power in favor of the platform regarding what communication can take place and how that communication can happen (Perel and Elkin-Koren 2017). Closedness regarding what the rules are and how they are applied, in other words, seems to serve the platform and not the public. In these arguments, openness about the rules of censure, rather than closedness, seems to be the better approach to misinformation.

On the other hand, when examined from the perspective of cultivating spaces that uphold epistemic responsibility, there may be pitfalls inherent to being open about the rules of censure, characterized by the technologies and techniques of twenty-first century, automation-enabled, internetworked communication. For example, "bots"—automated social media accounts—can be used to build numbers behind a particular claim of misinformation, relying on pre-programmed rules to operate (Coleman 2018a). The more transparent a given platform is about the rules, the more information actors have to work with to avoid detection, flagging, or removal. And, similarly, persons can also work from knowledge of the rules to operate around them, choosing for instance "coded" language to avoid detection on the platform. Knowing what the rules are help people to play the game fairly; but, there are people who are willing to exploit the rules at the expense of the public's ability to know well. Because gaming the rules is a feature of communication on the contemporary social web, it also constitutes a potential reason *for* closedness. Of course, as indicated above, there are also less noble possibilities of motive driving the closing off of access to the rules and processes of censure on social media platforms, moored in the idea of private companies protecting their own interests at the expense of the public's interests, for closedness seems to serve the platform by shielding its actions from reproach with opaque mechanisms.

Closedness and openness exist across a spectrum. Completely "open-source" approaches, which not only make rules of censure publicly available, but also the code and procedures used to apply those rules, would be the most open (but are also rare). Completely closed approaches, on the other hand, keep all rules of censure as well as code and procedures private, inaccessible to the general public (but completely closed systems are also rare). Most platforms exist somewhere between closed and open, making some rules, code, and/or procedures public, while keeping others hidden (e.g., the details of the automation used to detect misinformation).

Directionality: Top-Down and Bottom-Up Approaches

As a general intuition, in the United States at least, it seems a defensible claim that any and every person has the *right* to speak in the public sphere, even on technical matters of science (Coleman 2015). As such, *any* regulation of persons' abilities to speak publicly might strike some as a violation of freedom of speech. For instance, it is common for people to defend not the substance of what one says (e.g., "Vaccines will turn us into monkeys") but rather persons' rights to say something in the first place. Some may operate from these intuitions, guiding them to a view in which the cultivation of spaces for knowing well requires a "no holds barred" approach to communication on a given social media platform, allowing for any and everything to be said so as to uphold the appeal of freedom of expression. However, competing with the general appeal of unadulterated freedom of expression are the realities of the tactics used by conspiratorial actors who rely on building the impression that there is *more* to their arguments by leveraging appeals to freedom of speech and/or appeals to a "balanced" perspective in journalistic ethics to build legitimacy by garnering public attention, sometimes even leveraging automation to pad numbers of followers, or to jump claims of misinformation to the top of the social media feed (Ceccarelli 2011; Coleman 2018a). Another reality working against completely unregulated communication on social media platforms is that of online aggression, modes of communication that are ostensibly uninterested in connections between persons that might result in knowing well, and instead demonstrate attempts to silence, or cast out, fellow community members (Reyman and Sparby 2019). Online aggression manifests in such tactics as flaming, harassment, doxxing, hate speech, or other behaviors which are meant to inflict harm, rather than express ideas, in turn demonstrating a basic need for intervention in the form of enforcing ground rules of interaction (Reyman and Sparby 2019).

It may be a fairly easy claim to accept in recognizing that basic rules of interaction might be necessary on social media platforms (e.g., "do not misinform or use hate speech on this platform"). However, where things get sticky is in figuring the best methods for *defining* and *enforcing* those rules. There exist both top-down and bottom-up approaches. *Top-down* approaches leave definition and enforcement of the rules of governing speech to the administrators of a given social media platform. *Bottom-up* approaches, on the other hand, leave control to the broader user community, where the platform might facilitate definition and enforcement of the rules, but ultimately, it is born of the work of the user community.

Like the openness or closedness regarding transparency of rules of censure, the directionality of defining and enforcing those rules exists across a spectrum of top-down to bottom-up. Radically top-down approaches would excise the community from having any say in the rules or enforcement of censure. Radically bottom-up approaches, on the other hand, while relying on the platform to facilitate definition and enforcement of the rules, might nearly completely remove the platform from any direct say in the rules and how they are applied. Most platforms exist somewhere between radically top-down or bottom-up, wherein, for instance, a platform may hand down rules of censure defined by platform administrators but rely on users to flag or apply those rules so that they can be enforced. And, in a similar sense of both-and, some platforms may present as bottom-up, while including implicit rules and enforcements actualized in the affordances and constraints of the platform itself (e.g., in not being able to post long-form explanations of science on a given platform due to video or text length limits).

Where bottom-up approaches to defining and enforcing rules might initially strike most people as the most desirable ones amid an infodemic in that they reflect a sort of "for the people, by the people" sensibility of governance, this is complicated by some recent scholarship, which indicates that people "who fall for fake news [misinformation] are also more receptive to pseudo-profound bullshit, more willing to overclaim knowledge, and score lower on the CRT [Cognitive Reflection Test] (a test of analytic thinking)" (Pennycook and Rand 2020, 197). The implication here is that one cannot presume that the general user community possesses the expertise necessary for identifying, and responding to misinformation, and so, perhaps a top-down approach, wherein platform administrators, in conversation with experts, define the rules and oversee their enforcement, emerges as the desirable approach. On top of this, the use of community-based affordances for identifying and responding to problematic posts can be used by actors to harass other users (regardless of the epistemic merit of their content), a problem inherent to community enforcement of censure.

Of course, there are more nuanced ways to move forward from such an implication that attempts to control misinformation while preserving some semblance of democratic participation, while intersecting with approaches to the transparency of defining and enforcing rules. For example, top-down approaches, which take more open approaches to make accessible the discussions that led to a particular post being removed, offer one such nuanced approach, which, in Kate Crawford and Tarleton Gillespie's (2016) view,

> might involve a space for "backstage" discussion, one that preserved the history of debates about a particular video, image, or post. This would provide a space for engaged debate where objections and counter-objections could be made, rather than the current process, which is inscrutable to other users. This could also allow some complaints to be worked out without site interference, such as when a complaint is withdrawn or an argument is conceded. Users could see where complaints had previously occurred and been rejected, with explanations from the site's policy team when possible, saving them time and uncertainty in the long run. Finally, even if content is removed, debate about it could remain and continue.... Significantly, it would offer a space for people to articulate their concerns, which works against both algorithmic and human gaming of the system to have content removed. (422–23)

In such an approach, ultimately, it is left to platform administrators to remove a given post, but one informed by the community's flagging of content in conjunction to "above board" discussions of a given decision, representing a more sophisticated approach to the directionality of decision-making on a platform, intersecting with transparency in ways that attempt to navigate the problem of misinformation. But, to tie to the competing demands of dialogue and expediency noted earlier, such a process, while it demonstrates a value for dialogue, might also represent a process that chafes against the urgency to act quickly, especially amid an infodemic, where the problem is not just about the *quality* of information but also the *quantity*.

In light of a 2020 study by Kouzy et al. that demonstrated that 24.8 percent of all the Twitter posts analyzed contained misinformation—virtually a quarter of all posts about COVID-19 analyzed in the study—the problem of scale is manifest. And, thus, automation emerges as a component of the process of identifying and responding to misinformation, a complicating factor that often involves top-down definitions, hidden in a black box of code, which, at least ostensibly, can be applied in the spirit of cultivating spaces of knowing well. As Dietram Scheufele and Nicole Krause (2019) observe in the context of science misinformation, and specifically the use of automated detection and censure technologies:

Implicitly, most approaches to algorithmic curation of facts assume that citizens are misinformed because they are unable to sift through and critically evaluate information in emerging (social) media environments. There is no doubt that low levels of media literacy among citizens are part of the problem. (7664)

The observation draws out that, in response to the sheer scale of misinformation, in combination with the notion that publics might not possess the literacy necessary for identifying and responding to misinformation, top-down automation might emerge as a viable means for upholding epistemic responsibility. But, in contrast to this view, it could be argued that automation problematically simplifies the process of knowing well, a process moored in open discussion, and aimed at teasing out the nuances of truth between persons. Tarleton Gillespie (2020) raises such an issue, by hedging a critique situated in the idea that automating content regulation is to problematically presume a static vision of what truth is or how truth should be expressed, when in fact, those things are discovered in dialogue. Gillespie is careful to note that "penalizing someone for violating the rules is in fact one of the ways we as communities and societies discover, test, and reassert our shared values," but while noting that "there is no stable, widely shared value system that simply must be implemented" (3). So, where the cultivation of spaces of knowing well amid an infodemic on the social web is concerned, there might be reasons to use automation in that it offers an expedient route to controlling misinformation. But there also exist reasons to forgo its use, for it might problematically perpetuate singular definitions of what counts as dialogue, constraining the means by which knowing well can happen in the first place.

While the discussion thus far is certainly not exhaustive of the pragmatic and ethical trade-offs of different approaches to the transparency and directionality of rules of censure in platformed responses to misinformation during an infodemic, it does draw out some of the competing values of dialogue and expediency in tension amid platformed responses to misinformation during an infodemic. Some platforms prioritize expediency, and others prioritize dialogue, manifested in varying procedural performances regarding the cultivation of spaces of knowing well, describable across a matrix of closed/open and top-down/bottom-up approaches. The coming analysis will offer some discussion and examples of "in-between" situations. For example, the ways in which appeals to expert dialogue might be leveraged to close off dialogue to the broader public in the context of the COVID-19 pandemic, representing a *sort of* bottom-up approach, which is open, but in a limited way. Before the analysis, though, I will first summarize the matrix in table 1.1.

Table 1.1 Matrix of "Platformed" Responses to Misinformation

	Top-Down	Bottom-Up
Open	The rules of moderation are *transparent*, but unaffected by users. Rules of moderation are *defined and enforced by the platform*, independently of users.	The rules of moderation are *transparent* and derived from user input. Rules of moderation are *defined and enforced by the user community* but facilitated by the platform.
Closed	The rules of moderation are *hidden* and unaffected by users. Rules of moderation are *defined and enforced by the platform*, independently of users.	The rules of moderation are *hidden* but derived from user input. Rules of moderation are *defined and enforced by the user community* but facilitated by the platform.

APPLYING THE MATRIX OF "PLATFORMED" RESPONSES TO MISINFORMATION

To examine the implications of various platformed interventions into misinformation, I will draw on public documentation regarding misinformation policies of specific social media platforms. From these documents, I will describe the approach of each platform with attention to whether the platform's approach is open or closed and top-down or bottom-up, while considering the apparent valuing of expediency or dialogue represented in that approach, and the implications of that approach to the cultivation of space for knowing well amid the COVID-19 infodemic. Rather than attempt a comprehensive analysis (which would be of substantial length, for there are numerous social media platforms), the analysis will instead highlight the usefulness of the matrix of transparency and directionality in platformed responses to misinformation by focusing on three major media platforms—Reddit, YouTube, and Twitter—which each employ unique approaches.

Reddit

The format of Reddit is individual threads, which often center on a topic or shared interest, manifesting as a "subreddit." These threads are moderated by volunteer members of the Reddit community, who, in many ways, are responsible for the definition and enforcement of rules of censure on a given subreddit. However, Reddit nonetheless describes more global rules that are pertinent to the mitigation of misinformation on the platform.

Reddit does not have a misinformation policy per se, but it does have a "quarantine" policy, wherein a "community" (also known as a "subreddit")

will be assigned a warning message displayed to users before they can access a specific subreddit. Quarantines are applied based on offensive content or content that perpetuates "hoaxes." The language from the Reddit quarantine policy:

> There will sometimes be communities that, while not prohibited, average redditors may nevertheless find highly offensive or upsetting. In other cases, communities may be dedicated to promoting hoaxes (yes we used that word) that warrant additional scrutiny, as there are some things that are either verifiable or falsifiable and not seriously up for debate. In these circumstances, Reddit Administrators may apply a quarantine. (Reddit 2022d)

As explained in the policy, moderators (persons responsible for overseeing a given community/subreddit) who feel that they have been unfairly assigned quarantine status can submit an appeal, revealing that there is some answerability to decisions made by platform administrators, even if it is not necessarily as open as a Wikipedia model, where the discussions about the decision to quarantine are also brandished publicly. One could characterize Reddit's quarantine policy as one that is top-down, facilitated by community reporting and textured by a process of appeal. Consequently, although the rules are fairly clear in the policy, the process itself is less clear (e.g., how it is that a given rule is applied in a specific case).

On a cursory read, Reddit's quarantine policy largely reads as harboring a reluctance to *ban* a community on the basis of "hoaxy" content, reserving banning instead for violations of Reddit's general content policy, which disallows content or behavior that promotes hate or violence; manipulation of the platform (e.g., spamming or subscriber fraud); violations of user privacy; sexual content regarding minors; deceptive impersonation; mistagging graphic, offensive, or sexually explicit content; illegal transactions; or interfering with the normal operation of the platform (Reddit 2022e). Consequently, the rules can be said to prioritize dialogue over expediency in that they are designed to support connecting well (the rules for banning largely have to do with online aggression and/or disruption of the platform itself), offering some form of a barrier between the general public and a quarantined subreddit, as a means of facilitating knowing well while upholding an apparent value for freedom of expression. Interestingly though, the only discernible mention of the word "misinformation" in the Reddit policy documentation regards a clause included in the elaboration on the rule to "not post violent content." Following a bulleted list forbidding such things as threats of violence or violent propaganda, the policy states: "Note that health misinformation, namely falsifiable health information that encourages or poses a significant risk of physical harm to the reader, also violates the Rule" (Reddit 2022c). And, although not explicit in the policy per se, a post made by Reddit administrators clarifies that, in light of COVID-19 denialism, a similar extension of a broader content rule is extended specifically to disinformation, by clarifying that the rule to "not impersonate a person or entity" (Reddit 2022b) will be interpreted "as covering health disinformation, meaning falsifiable health information that has been manipulated and presented to mislead. This includes falsified medical data and faked WHO/CDC advice" (Reddit 2022a).

In this light, it seems that, despite the general prioritization of dialogue that characterizes Reddit's content policy, when it comes to health misinformation, such as that which characterizes the COVID-19 infodemic, the value of expedience takes rein, upheld by a definition of health misinformation as violence. In turn, the platform's unique approach to cultivating a space of knowing seems to rhetorically negotiate the preservation of a broader commitment to public expression and dialogue (e.g., in moves toward quarantining rather than banning) while allowing for expedient response to health misinformation, seemingly under a rubric of protecting publics from violence and deception. Misinformation about COVID-19 is shaped in the documents to be something antithetical to dialogue and thus requiring expedience.

YouTube

YouTube's format is that of individual "channels," or video blog accounts, usually controlled by one person or entity (e.g., a company). In contrast to Reddit, which seems to err on the side of quarantine, rather than banning or removing content, YouTube seems to err in the other direction.

YouTube has a specific misinformation policy, which threatens direct removal of content that "promotes dangerous remedies or cures," "suppression of census participation," "manipulated content," or "misattributed content" (YouTube 2022b). A YouTube account found to engage in any of these behaviors, according to the policy, will be given an initial warning. Any subsequent violations will result in a "strike" against that account. Three strikes within ninety days will result in termination of an account. The policy is a top-down approach, facilitated by automation. According to the Frequently Asked Questions page for YouTube's community guidelines enforcement,

> YouTube's automated flagging systems start working as soon as a user attempts to publish a video or post a comment. The content is scanned by machines to assess whether it may violate YouTube's Community Guidelines. YouTube also utilizes automated systems to prevent re-uploads of known violative content, including through the use of hashes (or "digital fingerprints"). (YouTube 2022c)

In congruence to this, while not contained in the misinformation policy directly, it is also explained that automation is used to afford necessary context to videos about COVID-19:

> Health source information panels on videos to help viewers identify videos from authoritative sources, and health content shelves that more effectively highlight videos from these sources when you search for specific health topics. These context cues are aimed at helping people more easily navigate and evaluate credible health information. (Graham 2021)

While YouTube clarifies that the machines do not make the ultimate decision to remove a post or assign a strike, but rather that humans make those decisions, the approach to misinformation on the platform is a top-down approach, facilitated in part by community flagging in combination with proprietary algorithms, which adds an additional layer of opacity to the process of censuring specific content. Similar to Reddit, although YouTube users have the option to appeal a given strike, representing a basic form of answerability, that process itself is not publicly accessible.

Beyond a general misinformation policy, YouTube also has a specific COVID-19 misinformation policy, which defines COVID-19 misinformation as anything that "contradicts local health authorities' (LHA) or the World Health Organization's (WHO) medical information about COVID-19" regarding "treatment," "prevention," "diagnosis," "transmission," "social distancing and self-isolation guidelines," and the "existence of COVID-19" (YouTube 2022a). The definition of COVID-19 misinformation as that which steps out of the bounds of external institutions such as the WHO or the CDC is a move that positions the rules of censure beyond the platform administration in a manner that, at least prima facie, seems to be a more bottom-up approach in the sense of mooring one's definitions in public sector institutions, affording some semblance of community governance over the definition of misinformation. Ultimately, though, those rules are applied by the platform, and not the broader user community itself, representing a dialogic approach, but one applied in an expedient fashion. Put differently, the approach upholds epistemic responsibility by outlining rules that recognize the expertise that results from dialogue among experts, but which are *applied* at the discretion of platform administrators. The implications which are represented in an adaptation of the three-strikes rule of the general misinformation policy, which adds to the COVID-19 misinformation policy, the statement that "severe abuse, or when the channel is dedicated to a policy violation," can result in direct termination of an account (YouTube 2022a). Where Reddit negotiates a broader commitment to dialogue (over expediency), making a special case for health information to allow for expedient response to misinformation, YouTube operates from a broader commitment to expediency, but one that uniquely appeals to expert dialogue, beyond the platform itself in cases of COVID-19 misinformation to facilitate added expediency. Defining the rules of censure beyond YouTube, by mooring those rules in such public institutions as the WHO or the CDC, moreover, affords a sense of communal authority to the rules, which supports specific applications of additionally expedient action in cases of health misinformation (like skipping the three-strikes rule).

Twitter

Micro-blogging, the format of Twitter, involves user accounts (e.g., @ scienceperson), which include "Tweets," or short-form commentary and statements as well as "hashtags" or identifiers added to individual Tweets to thread them together around a shared topic or issue (e.g., #covidvaccine). Twitter's approach can be characterized as existing between Reddit's broader reluctance to ban or remove content and YouTube's more restrictive, and largely automated, enforcement of censure.

Twitter's COVID-19 misinformation policy describes an array of responses to misinformation, applied at the discretion of system administrators, based on the assessed degree of rules transgression. For example, content removal is reserved for "severely harmful" tweets that: "advance a claim of fact, expressed in definitive terms"; are "demonstrably false or misleading, based on widely available, authoritative sources"; and are "likely to impact public safety or cause serious harm" (Twitter 2022c). But, alongside content removal, the "labeling" of misinformed Tweets is described as a potential response, ostensibly applied in cases of misunderstandings or misinterpretations of science rather than full-out science denialism (although, based on the documents it is difficult to tell how this policy would be applied). In cases of labeling a Tweet, this could involve "presenting a warning message on the Tweet," "showing an additional prompt to warn people before sharing or liking the Tweet," "reducing visibility of the Tweet on Twitter and/or preventing it from being recommended," "turning off likes, replies, and Retweets," or "providing a link to additional explanations or clarifications, such as in a curated landing page or relevant Twitter policies" (Twitter 2022c). In clarifying what does *not* count as removable, or labelable, misinformation, the policy seems to hinge on the difference between claims of fact and claims of opinion, explaining that "commentary, opinions, and satire," as well as "campaigns against official advisories or recommendations," "counterspeech," "personal anecdotes," and "debate about the advancement of COVID-19 science and research," would be instances in which the misinformation policy would not be violated (Twitter 2022c).

The rules themselves seem to attempt to walk the line between upholding freedom of expression, on balance with the potential harms of dangerous information (e.g., in protecting opinions, but scrutinizing statements of fact). And, those rules are fairly clear, representing some amount of transparency on what counts, or not, as misinformation on the platform. However, like Reddit and YouTube, while one might have a fairly good idea of what the rules are, the process in which those rules are defined and applied is much less clear.

Twitter's definition and enforcement of the rules implies a top-down approach, and one perhaps even more top-down than YouTube when considering that YouTube relies more on community flagging than Twitter does. While there exists a mechanism for reporting misinformation by the general user community in some countries, largely the enforcement of the policy happens "in close coordination with trusted partners including public health authorities, NGOs and governments" (Twitter 2022c) and is actualized through the "leverage[ing] [of] proactive detection using a combination of keyword heuristics and machine learning models to identify harmful forms of COVID-19 related misleading information" (Twitter 2022c).

Beyond removing and labeling content, Twitter also employs a strike system at the account level (i.e., two strikes for violations that result in Tweet removal; one strike for Tweets that require labeling). Enforcement action ranges from "no account-level action" for a single strike, on up to a "12-hour account lock" for two-to-three strikes, a "7-day account lock" for four strikes, and "permanent suspension" for accounts with more than five strikes (Twitter 2022c). It is noted that accounts that "misrepresent their affiliation, or share content that falsely represents its affiliation as a medical practitioner, public health official or agency, research institution, or that falsely suggests expertise on COVID-19 issues" as well as accounts that have "been set up with the expressed purpose of Tweeting false or misleading information about COVID-19" will be directly suspended (Twitter 2022c). Users are afforded the option to submit an appeal if they feel their account has been erroneously locked or suspended. While there is some form of answerability in the form of an appeal process, the heavy reliance on automation used to detect and respond to questionable content, in conjunction with the internal evaluations regarding what the rules are and how the rules should be enforced, adds opacity to Twitter's process. Twitter, while offering a much more transparent explanation of what the rules are, nonetheless keeps the discussions and processes of different outcomes (e.g., removal or labeling) from view, demonstrating a similar opacity to that of Reddit and YouTube. Moreover, like YouTube and Reddit, Twitter negotiates the need for dialogue, but in a way that frames misinformation about COVID-19 as subject to expedient action. In contrast to Reddit, Twitter positions misinformation in the broader realm of harm (but does not necessarily frame it as "violence"), while retaining an option to "label" (which is similar to "quarantining"). In comparison to YouTube, Twitter demonstrates a similar commitment to mitigating the problems of misinformed "facts" in a top-down manner while mooring its decision-making in broader dialogue of experts working in coalition with communally authoritative organizations, but adds a specific valuation of public "opinion" in the form of rules that distinguish between expressions of opinion and statements of fact.

CONCLUSION

In synthesis of the analysis of Reddit, YouTube, and Twitter's misinformation policies, it can be said that all three platforms, while in some ways transparent in what the rules are, largely keep hidden the processes of how those rules are applied in specific cases. We can also say that all three platforms, even those that seem broadly reluctant to remove content, demonstrate platformed responses that tend to value expediency in the context of an infodemic, such as the COVID-19 pandemic. Put in terms of cultivating spaces for knowing well, the responsibility being heeded by these social media platforms exists in protecting publics from misinformation, defined either as "violence" or "deception," and/or that which is out of step with publicly recognized institutions of health science, and constitutes incorrect claims of fact (rather than an opinion).

While such approaches demonstrate effort on the part of social media platforms to exercise epistemic responsibility in the form of action to cultivate spaces in which knowing well can take place, a question could also be raised regarding the *necessity* of opaque processes and top-down decision-making. That is, the analysis tells us that Reddit, YouTube, and Twitter are operating from perspectives in which expediency should override dialogue in the context of a public health crisis. And, based on the earlier discussion of the potential ethical and pragmatic trade-offs of different approaches, there exist reasons for such approaches. Processes of applying rules (including automated algorithms) might be kept hidden in efforts to avoid equipping some actors with information useful for gaming the system as well as to protect the proprietary information of a private company from public view. Similarly, in the context of misinformation, where one might not be able to trust that the general public has the science literacy to participate in the definition and enforcement of the rules, a top-down approach, informed by dialogue among experts, might emerge as potentially better than a more bottom-up approach based in the general user community. Dialogue takes time, which perhaps is not in abundance during a public health crisis, and, so, expedience takes the reins during the COVID-19 pandemic. But, ethically speaking, epistemic responsibility is something that should spring up from the work of a *community*. And, pragmatically, some science conspiracists can leverage nontransparent instances of informational censure to garner legitimacy for their projects. As such, there are very good reasons to continue to probe possibilities of platformed response to misinformation on the social web.

What are the benefits or pitfalls of crowdsourcing misinformation identification, response, and commentary from the *community*, rather than getting it from the *platform*, for instance? Twitter's Birdwatch, currently offered as an exploratory extension of the Twitter platform, allows users to add notes to specific Tweets, offering corrections and context for instances of misinformation (Coleman 2021). Users' notes can then be voted on by other users marking them as helpful, or not. In a seemingly radical move toward transparency, the source code for Birdwatch's algorithms, which calculate reputation and consensus tracking, is even offered up to users for public input (Twitter 2022a). While such an approach to misinformation represents a staunchly bottom-up approach, enabled by radical transparency, the approach might also introduce new barriers to knowing well, moored in online aggression and manifested in the targeting of commentators based on such things as identity, rather than the merits of a given claim (Reyman and Sparby 2019). Twitter has attempted to adapt the platform to afford users the opportunity to use an "alias," or an automatically generated pseudonym assigned to a given user, affording an avenue for making accountability possible, while protecting users from abuse, or even encouraging discussion beyond partisanship (e.g., by avoiding markers of political affiliation) (Twitter 2022b). Such seems to be a sensible approach to the need to connect well while engaging in the activity of knowing well. But, overall, Birdwatch also raises a pragmatic question regarding the centrality of expertise to discussions of science misinformation (e.g., "You're not a scientist!" or "You're not a *real* scientist!"). Consequently, where valuing expediency over dialogue, as was described in the earlier examples, seems imperfect, so, too, does the model of valuing dialogue over expediency, at least in the context of a public health crisis being deliberated on the social web. Rather than attempt to make a case for the best approach, it is probably better to conclude with the idea that identifying and evaluating misinformation on social media during an infodemic is a task that requires nuanced approaches to the competing demands of expediency and dialogue.

REFERENCES

Bogost, Ian. 2007. *Persuasive Games: The Expressive Power of Videogames*. Cambridge: MIT Press.

Brock, Kevin, and Dawn Shepherd. 2016. "Understanding How Algorithms work Persuasively through the Procedural Enthymeme." *Computers and Composition* 42: 17–27.

Ceccarelli, Leah. 2011. "Manufactured Scientific Controversy: Science, Rhetoric, and Public Debate." *Rhetoric and Public Affairs* 14, no. 2: 195–228.
Code, Lorraine. 2020. *Epistemic Responsibility*. Albany, NY: SUNY Press.
Coleman, Keith. 2021, January 25. "Introducing Birdwatch, a Community-Based Approach to Misinformation." *Twitter Blog*. https://blog.twitter.com/en_us/topics/product/2021/introducing-birdwatch-a-community-based-approach-to-misinformation.
Coleman, Miles C. 2015. "Courage and Respect in New Media Science Communication." *Journal of Media Ethics* 30, no. 3: 186–202.
———. 2017. "Rhetorical Logic Bombs and Fragmented Online Publics of Vaccine Science." *Journal of Contemporary Rhetoric* 7, no. 4: 203–16.
———. 2018a. "Bots, Social Capital, and the Need for Civility." *Journal of Media Ethics* 33, no. 3: 120–32.
———. 2018b. "The Role of Patience in Arguments about Vaccine Science." *Western Journal of Communication* 82, no. 4: 513–28.
Coleman, Miles C., and Joy M. Cypher. 2020. "The Digital Rhetorics of AIDS Denialist Networked Publics." *First Monday* 25, no. 10: 1–15.
Cotter, Kelley, Julia R. DeCook, and Shaheen Kanthawala. 2022. "Fact-Checking the Crisis: COVID-19, Infodemics, and the Platformization of Truth." *Social Media+Society* 8, no. 1: 1–13.
Crawford, Kate, and Tarleton Gillespie. 2016. "What Is a Flag For? Social Media Reporting Tools and the Vocabulary of Complaint." *New Media & Society* 18, no. 3: 410–28.
Etzioni, Amitai. 2019. "Should We Privatize Censorship?" *Issues in Science and Technology* 36, no. 1: 19–22.
Gillespie, Tarleton. 2018. *Custodians of the Internet*. New Haven, CT: Yale University Press.
———. 2020. "Content Moderation, AI, and the Question of Scale." *Big Data & Society* 7, no. 2: 1–5.
Graham, Garth. 2021. "Introducing New Ways to Help You Find Answers to Your Health Questions." *YouTube Official Blog*, July 19. https://blog.YouTube/news-and-events/introducing-new-ways-help-you-find-answers-your-health-questions.
Hintz, Arne. 2015. "Social Media Censorship, Privatised Regulation and New Restrictions to Protest and Dissent." In *Critical Perspectives on Social Media Protest: Between Control and Emancipation*, edited by Lina Dencik and Oliver Leistert. Lanham, MD: Rowman & Littlefield.
Kendall-Taylor, Andrea, Erica Frantz, and Joseph Wright. 2020. "The Digital Dictators: How Technology Strengthens Autocracy." *Foreign Affairs* 99, no. 2: 103–15.
Kouzy, Ramez, Joseph Abi Jaoude, Afif Kraitem, Molly B. El Alam, Basil Karam, Elio Adib, Jabra Zarka, Cindy Traboulsi, Elie W. Akl, and Khalil Baddour. 2020. "Coronavirus Goes Viral: Quantifying the COVID-19 Misinformation Epidemic on Twitter." *Cureus* 12, no. 3: 1–9.
Nyhan, Brendan, and Jason Reifler. 2010. "When Corrections Fail: The Persistence of Political Misperceptions." *Political Behavior* 32, no. 2: 303–30.

Pennycook, Gordon, and David G. Rand. 2020. "Who Falls for Fake News? The Roles of Bullshit Receptivity, Overclaiming, Familiarity, and Analytic Thinking." *Journal of Personality* 88, no. 2: 185–200.

Perel, Maayan, and Niva Elkin-Koren. 2017. "Black Box Tinkering: Beyond Disclosure in Algorithmic Enforcement." *Florida Law Review* 69, no. 1: 181–222.

Pröllochs, Nicolas. 2021. "Community-Based Fact-Checking on Twitter's Birdwatch Platform." *arXiv preprint arXiv:2104.07175*.

Reddit. 2022a. "COVID-19 Denialism and Policy Clarifications." r/redditsecurity. www.reddit.com/r/redditsecurity/comments/pfyqqn/covid_denialism_and_policy_clarifications.

———. 2022b. "Do Not Impersonate a Person or Entity. Rules & Reporting." www.reddithelp.com/hc/en-us/articles/360043075032.

———. 2022c. "Do Not Post Violent Content." Rules & Reporting. www.reddithelp.com/hc/en-us/articles/360043513151-Do-not-post-violent-content.

———. 2022d. "Quarantined Subreddits." Rules & Reporting. www.reddithelp.com/hc/en-us/articles/360043069012-Quarantined-Subreddits.

———. 2022e. "Rules." Content Policy. www.redditinc.com/policies/content-policy.

Reyman, Jessica, and Erika M. Sparby, eds. 2019. *Digital Ethics: Rhetoric and Responsibility in Online Aggression*. New York: Routledge.

Scheufele, Dietram A., and Nicole M. Krause. 2019. "Science Audiences, Misinformation, and Fake News." *Proceedings of the National Academy of Sciences* 116, no. 16: 7662–69.

Suzor, Nicolas P., Sarah Myers West, Andrew Quodling, and Jillian York. 2019. "What Do We Mean When We Talk About Transparency? Toward Meaningful Transparency in Commercial Content Moderation." *International Journal of Communication* 13: 1526–43.

Twitter. 2022a. "Birdwatch." *GitHub*. Accessed January 30, 2022, at https://github.com/twitter/birdwatch.

———. 2022b. "Birdwatch Aliases." *Birdwatch Guide*. https://twitter.github.io/birdwatch/contributing/aliases.

———. 2022c. "COVID-19 Misleading Information Policy." Platform Integrity and Authenticity. https://help.twitter.com/en/rules-and-policies/medical-misinformation-policy.

Vraga, Emily K., and Leticia Bode. 2017. "Using Expert Sources to Correct Health Misinformation in Social Media." *Science Communication* 39, no. 5: 621–45.

World Health Organization. 2020, April 15. *Coronavirus Disease 2019 (COVID-19) Situation Report*. No. 86. https://web.archive.org/web/20210308172123/www.who.int/docs/default-source/coronaviruse/situation-reports/20200415-sitrep-86-covid-19.pdf.

YouTube. 2022a. "COVID-19 Medical Misinformation Policies." Misinformation Policies. https://support.google.com/YouTube/answer/9891785?hl=en&ref_topic=10833358.

———. 2022b. "Misinformation Policies." YouTube Policies. https://support.google.com/YouTube/answer/10834785?hl=en&ref_topic=10833358.

———. 2022c. "YouTube Community Guidelines Enforcement FAQs." Transparency Report Help Center. https://support.google.com/transparencyreport/answer/9209072.

Chapter 2

Hashtag Populism

Plandemics, Scamdemics, and Viral Resistance

Linda Howell

At the time of the writing of this essay, a social movement calling itself the Freedom Convoy was making its way across Canada. The convoy blocked borders and occupied cities such as Vancouver and Ottawa to protest local and national vaccination and mask mandates and fashioned its message as one of resistance to tyranny. This convoy employs a disruptive protest tactic because its position both in cities and at the country's borders stressed the already struggling supply chain issues facing North America, as a result of the COVID-19 pandemic (Pruitt-Young 2022).

This seemingly successful disruptive tactic inspired calls for similar protests, most notably in the United States and France. These calls to action were spurred by controversies surrounding local, regional/state, and national regulations, mandates, and guidelines for how to operate daily in a pandemic-plagued world; the reliance on the "trucker" and the "farmer" as iconic representations of the movement is important to note here, as the protest rhetoric around mandates has been driven, in large part, by a social class frame as well as a geographic frame, especially in terms of rural versus urban areas (Sanchez-Paramo 2020). From the earliest stages of the COVID-19 pandemic in January 2020, media and social media feeds concocted a narrative of disingenuity around institutional approaches to the spread of the pandemic, often nurturing stories of injustice and unfairness that many populist groups and personalities have taken up as their banners of action.

The key theme that emerges from the populist frustration is the perception that one population of citizens is being asked to do things that another is not. One way to capture this frustration and to see how it gets fed and feeds itself is to look toward popular avenues of communication, and in this essay,

I will focus on Twitter and two hashtags: #scamdemic and #plandemic. The evolution of these tags demonstrates how narratives of conspiracy collide with lines of political resistance, and in so doing, allows us to see some of the stories around which people are gathering. These stories operate on key rhetorical devices, most notably antonomasia and hyperbole, wherein some participants who do not trust the institutional responses to the COVID-19 health crisis have renamed the pandemic and those same participants have used that renaming as a platform to provide an alternative and grand narrative about the global response. The use of these rhetorical devices yields an opportunity to analyze how these hashtags construct a system of distribution in which the sharing of information, even misinformation, can affect or even shape our current reality.

BACKGROUND AND MOTIVATION FOR EXAMINATION

In his book *On Rumors: How Falsehoods Spread, Why We Believe Them, and What Can Be Done,* Cass Sunstein (2014) notes that "most rumors involve topics on which people lack direct or personal knowledge, and so most of us defer to the crowd" (19). This structure is in many ways the structure of expertise—the reliance on authority to understand something about the world, but in this case, rumor and gossip stand in for a type of authority, the authority of the masses. There is a seduction to the *ad populum* appeal, a sense of belonging that comes with going with the crowd, and it is in this vein that rumor and gossip may provide readers an avenue of access to the question of how and why we often believe hearsay, or they say, but such spread goes beyond consumption of information into the production and distribution of information.

Authority rests on authentication, and these hashtags demonstrate a type of authentication process that has become increasingly familiar in the social media landscape: group meaning-making. Such a structure harkens back to what Mieke Bal (1994) sees as part of the work of narratology and how signs and sign events contribute to the structures of meaning (19–22). Further, Bal's work in understanding the affective power of self-portraiture provides a frame for this examination (129). I would like to note here that I want to avoid psychologizing the hashtags and the hashtag participants; however, there is a wealth of information and analysis to be found in underscoring the affective or pathic power of the discourse and how those hashtags contribute to that overwhelmingly emotional narrative.

Both Sunstein (2014) and Bal (1994) offer a gateway into the significance of this type of study, but the theoretical frames this essay uses come in three forms which I will discuss in the methodology section: metanarrative, convergence culture, and antifandom. Each leg of this three-legged chair provides a perspective on the hows and wheres such misinformation forms and spreads. Here we must disentangle misinformation from itself to a degree. Misinformation casts a particular shade on what many participants in the hashtags see as the truth and/or the truth revealed. This type of transcendentalizing narrative complicates the expert/authority with student/citizen relationship. The inherent cynicism embedded in the hashtags reveals a disenchanted public who searches for the malevolent in many state or organizational level moves, decisions, and initiatives.

METHODOLOGY

Theory

This essay employs three theoretical frameworks for the examination and analysis of the case studies, which focus on sample tweets and accompanying links that emerge from those postings. The primary frame will be provided by metanarrative with the secondary areas being spreadable media and antifandom, specifically in the social media context. I chose these frameworks because they allow us to consider the complex infrastructure at play in creating, deploying, and sharing messaging, and how the distribution of information often gets tied to identity formation.

Metanarrative/Metafiction

When Lyotard (1989) wrote of metanarrative he noted that the evolution of knowledge acquisition and sharing was moving away from traditional ideas of training to a consumer/producer model, and thus the structure of that system would be inevitably altered. Metanarrative, or a grand narrative, provided meaning to modern societies, and it is the postmodern obligation, to a large degree, to view these narratives with what he notes as incredulity (xxiv, 4). The apparatus of the grand narrative can be seen across many different cultural, social, political, and other "large scale" populace contexts, but for the purpose of this work, I employ this theory as a way to see how social media has helped reconstruct the environs within which a grand narrative can take place and take place rapidly, wherein participants who actively spread and proselytize conspiracy theories around COVID-19 are attempting to construct a contemporary and contemporaneous grand narrative that gives meaning and symbolic value to the ordinary and mundane.

The grand narrative we see in the #scamdemic and #plandemic case studies are buttressed by two infrastructures of distribution. By understanding how media spreads and understanding and identifying an architecture for such spreading, we can begin to see how what appears rhizomatic and organic is manipulated, designed, and open to participation. What we will find in these postings and in the general outlay of the narrative are types of metafictional devices found in a long range and tradition of literary work such as parody and self-reflexive narrative. Parody, as Krista Giappone (2015) argues, can be seen as a "counter-genre," a call back to Rose's (1993) work on parody. While Giappone focuses on the use of such humor in video games, the idea of engaging in counter-genre tactics works well when thinking about the almost reflexive metanarrative and metafictional spaces social media can provide and encourage. Parody is a popular postmodern invocation, but its uses go beyond simple humor, often being actively engaged with as a tool of criticism. With such devices, the possibilities of content creation and consumption can become even more engaging and, in spheres where participation is nursed, the spread can seem rhizomatic.

Convergence Culture

Henry Jenkins (2006) coined the term *convergence culture* as a conceptualization of the emergent mediascapes occupied by fans and other participatory cultures. Convergence culture denotes a media culture that sees the intersection of the social, economic, political, and technological converge and where "consumers are encouraged to seek out new information and make connections among dispersed media content" (3). For the purpose of this essay, I will use convergence culture, especially the idea of spreadable media, to understand the environs within which media commentary happens and how hashtags can create an immersive experience. In this case, the immersion is one tied to the creation and distribution of information about COVID-19 and the ramifications of such spread.

In 2013, Ford, Jenkins, and Green developed the idea of spreadable media as an antidote to the idea of an unwilling or vulnerable population being "infected" with viral marketing, underscoring that the Dawkinsian concept of the meme which draws from the Greek word *mimeme*, or mime, and its transmission does not provide an adequate model for understanding how media spreads or how audiences participate in that spreading (Dawkins 1976, 192). This model extended the work of convergence culture toward an industrial lens, highlighting how consumers create, distribute, and in many ways, self-authorize content.

This structure of content creation pushes back against the idea of passive consumption of media products but also points to the increasing corporatization of participatory culture (i.e., fandoms) that has been a consequence of the seeming democratization of social media. The ability of content creators and producers to have more immediate and intimate relationships (often superficial) demands a reconceptualization of the media landscape. The increasingly prominent role of public personas, both in traditional celebrity and the emergent influencer class, create and/or contribute to a façade of authenticity and seeming expertise of the public persona.

Antifandom and Impression Management

In his analysis of Television Without Pity (TWoP), Jonathan Gray (2005) defined *antifandom* as the "active and vocal dislike or hate of a program, genre, or personality," a claim he further explores in the 2019 collection *Antifandom: Dislike and Hate in the Digital Age* where he begins to categorize different types of antifandoms (anti-fans, bad objects, hatewatching) (841; Gray 2019, 25). Antifandom represents a movement against the authorized, distributed version of a text, whether that is a story or person. In that same collection, Cornel Sandvoss explores the antifandom component of political communication, specifically with regard to online forums tied to the United States Tea Party movement and proposes such antifans engage in a "politics of against" (Sandvoss 2019, 131). It is through that lens I propose we read the hashtags, in part as a move against, rather than a building for. For this essay, antifandom sits within the context of impression management.

First developed by Erving Goffman (2021) in *The Presentation of Self in Everyday Life*, the model of impression management, wherein a person tries to control how others perceive them, has been used by communications and other professional fields to understand how people, organizations, and others represent themselves (8). Because impression management ties directly to a person's identity management and formation, it has become an especially useful tool in examining social media environments and their intersection with identity. Further, I contend that impression management helps in contextualizing the prominence of celebrity commentary on the pandemic as an authentication device and how it gets fed and enabled by a strain of antifandom that seeks to build against one authority with another. For the purposes of this essay, I am defining celebrity broadly, rather than in the vein of Hollywood stars or other traditional definitions. Because of the influencer class that has become prevalent on social media, celebrity can offer a way in which people are seen, the measure of fame or infamy, as you might have it, and while cultural commentary often comments on the challenges of surveillance, there is also the counternarrative of acknowledgment, recognition, and the seduction of being seen.

Data Collection and Examination

The central movement of this essay is a rhetorical analysis of the language and word choice in the top tier of social media engagement on the platform

Twitter using the hashtags #scamdemic and #plandemic, with and without the numerical denotation, as well as accompanying references to external media and social media feeds. This essay seeks to read two hashtags from various social media feeds in an attempt to understand how avenues of information generation and distribution hubs employ rhetorical devices that encourage community building and a counter-isolationist narrative, which seeks to find commonality within these tags, often hooking them together with hashtags such as #fakenews, #bigtech, and other tags that both aimed to be serious or to be darkly funny with pun structures.

The broad range of devices center around three moves: definition, comparison, and causal argument. These devices are developed and distributed through both textual and visual cues, as we will see in the case studies provided. From the outset, both hashtags included those who posted and reiterated conspiracy theories with two primary strains: pointing out the perceived hypocrisy of governmental and health communication guidelines to benefit big corporations and the perceived planning done by so-called malevolent actors such as Bill Gates, the United States Democratic Party, and the People's Republic of China. Many tweets came from accounts that have followers in the tens and hundreds of thousands, which exponentializes the reach beyond the retweet numbers, a measure of influence and engagement that I have not captured in this study but will note as part of the case studies.

I began the study by looking at two tiers of engagement on Twitter: 500 or more retweets and 1,000 or more retweets. I focused on Twitter because the venue is public. I included no postings from locked or discontinued accounts, to respect the expectation of privacy denoted by that choice. An interesting note for users here: the Twitter platform posts links to COVID-19 information at the top of the plandemic hashtag and automatically makes the search pandemic. A user has to choose to search plandemic with a link that states "search instead for plandemic"; however, the same approach is not used in the scamdemic tag.

The purpose here was to determine if there were patterns of diction and rhetorical devices that generate more engagement since retweets are considered more engaging than simple likes. I put a time frame on the study to focus on tweets generated between three time frames: February 2020–August 2020, January 2021–May 2021, and August 2021–November 2021. I chose these timeframes to capture major waves of the coronavirus spread: initial spread and lockdown, run up to vaccination distribution, and Delta wave observations.

As I reviewed the data, I further reduced the parameters in terms of timeframe, detecting a pattern of interaction around major themes including economic and medical cynicism, governmental oppression, infringement on basic human rights, and corruption and cronyism. After that review, I drilled down to four specific dates: July 29, 2020, August 19, 2020, February 19, 2021, and August 19, 2021. I chose these dates to capture the rhetoric on single days that connect to the release of authorized information such as data on deaths and infections.

As I analyzed the tweets, a series of metanarratives emerged that focused on an unfolding global conspiracy that uses panic, hyperbole, and misrepresentation of data as manipulation tactics, a planned assault on small business economy, and using the virus regulations as a weapon against the populace and its populist leaders including Donald Trump. There emerges a triad of iconic representations of the COVID-19 scam from the rhetoric: Trump, the vulnerable co-morbid versus a healthy public, and the isolated child.

Scamdemic

The first case study will focus on the scamdemic hashtag and the tweets without the demarcation. The scamdemic case study produces observations about people's conspiratorial skepticism and the tag tended to be used in the first wave and as the lockdowns in 2020 continued over the summer months. There is a small sampling in the time frame from January to August 2020, a slightly larger sampling from January to May 2021, and then a slightly smaller sampling for the final timeframe in the 500 retweets or more category.

Plandemic

The plandemic hashtag has slightly more traffic, which could be explained in part by the release of the two-part 2020 documentary *Plandemic*. Having been removed from popular distribution sites like Facebook, YouTube, and Google, the documentary laid the groundwork for a social media threading that centered around the more coherent narrative of big pharma, big tech, and governmental handholding that seeks to oppress the masses. In this hashtag, I focused my approach in a similar way. The plandemic hashtag and term search yielded hundreds of tweets, but, for the most part, the themes diverged slightly from the scamdemic tag in that the claims of worldwide conspiracy got attached to it early on and stayed with it through the life span of the examination.

CASE STUDY: #SCAMDEMIC/SCAMDEMIC

Early Use and Initial Spread

The hashtag #scamdemic emerged in the Twittersphere early in the pandemic, and it is connected to the early rhetoric that posed the coronavirus as a hoax to marry with other such hashtags like #fakenews. To underscore these connections, I will review three tweets from the initial political conversations about the coronavirus. These tweets are in response to posters with a large number of followers: Dana Milbank (@milbank) from the Washington Post, the United States Republican Party (@GOP), and Reuters (@reuters). The initial spread of the term embeds itself in the response of governmental institutions to the spread and provides a frame for how the term unfolds over its lifespan to the end of 2021.

In a popular tweet from Washington Post columnist Dana Milbank on February 28, 2020, that was retweeted approximately 31,000 times, quote tweeted approximately 5,300 times, and received over 149,000 likes, he noted that "Remember this moment: Trump, in South Carolina, just called coronavirus a 'hoax'" (@milbank, February 28, 2020). This tweet garnered one of the first tweets with the word *scamdemic* as applied to the coronavirus. The user mirrors Milbank's rhetorical gambit with, "Remember this word, 'Scamdemic'" (@drallenprevette, February 28, 2020). While the user who invoked the word had a limited number of followers, fewer than 500, their reply was not directly to Milbank but instead a reply to a conservative account with over 400,000 followers, demonstrating its initial origins in a particular far right or U.S. conservative rhetorical landscape.

The second tweet to take note of is a reply to a February 24, 2020, tweet by Reuters where the news organization posted a clip from the World Health Organization. One user noted that "Coronavirus is a #scamdemic and is being pumped up by the #fakenews media to crash the stock market and give Democrats a shot at the White House. #fakeflus" (@silencefranklin, February 28, 2020). The user would follow up with an unsourced data point about the number of daily deaths from the flu in China before the coronavirus spread. This rhetorical move demonstrates the clear connection to the fake news rhetoric that is popular in far right/right/far left political and rhetorical circles.

Finally, in a February 28, 2020, tweet by the Republican Party (@GOP), a video of President Donald Trump from South Carolina, as noted in the Milbank tweet, emphasizes the Democratic Party's politicization of the coronavirus. Again, a user with fewer than 500 followers replied with two hashtags: #ScamDemic and #PANIC (@g6anon, February 28, 2020). It is important to note here the capitalization to emphasize the "Demic," which implies an attempt at a pun structure, aligning with a specific invocation of humor that Gal (2019) calls collective context collapse, helping groups to mark boundaries for themselves (733).

I choose to begin the case study in this way for two reasons. First, the rhizomatic architecture of Twitter performs much the same way networks of gossip and rumor work: long and complicated strings of telephone game threads that create a system of knowledge sharing that creates obstacles to sourcing but also feed into a heightening line of rhetoric. Second, the term *scamdemic* is clearly (a) a politicized retort to the increasing criticism of the Trump administration's approach to the virus's outbreak and (b) an addendum to the thread of criticism around various mainstream media outlets that these users see as manufactured panic and fake news. These two strains of the pandemic master narrative distinguish it from the latter case study of the term *plandemic*.

To give you a sense of scale and rapidity, in January 2020, there were no tweets with the term *scamdemic* included. In February 2020, there were approximately twenty tweets with the term included and only five users who included it. On August 30, 2020, one single day, the term was included in approximately 1,000 tweets. The timeframe between January and August is littered with emergent strains of conspiracy theories.

Summer 2020

On June 29, 2020, a self-described reporter with the account @howleyreporter released a series of tweets and videos accusing Child Protective Services of being an arm of the government designed to imitate "patriot-citizens" and infringe on parental rights. The parental rights narrative is a rhetorical turn that the opposition to both state lockdowns and vaccination initiatives are affectively funded by. This user positioned parental rights against government regulation and then provided a grand narrative that indicts Microsoft CEO Bill Gates in a wide-ranging conspiracy that includes exposing citizens to COVID-19, pushing quarantine protocols, and preventing hydroxychloroquine treatment for financial gain. The thesis is that the government is not a protective agency or run by its people but rather an apparatus of control and intrusion that these citizen patriots must work against. In the same run of tweets on June 29, 2020, another user proposes more Bill Gates-centric critiques with memes that verge on the racist but asserts that the National Institute of Health, like Howley reported, has financial stakes in the Moderna vaccine.

The scamdemic hashtag and term give readers a peek into the complicated anti-vaccine movement early on, and its accompanying skepticism, perhaps even cynicism, about government-driven health initiatives. It also underscores a particular type of scientific literacy practice that calls into question things such as COVID-19 testing. The hashtag on July 29, 2020, also includes several anecdotes about people testing positive, then testing negative for the coronavirus, and people getting positive results for no test at all. The expectation that tests are infallible and any deviation from that infallibility is malicious is a misunderstanding of health-care protocols, yes, but deeper still is the resistance to the health-care system.

I make note of this day because it was a high traffic day around a CDC update on COVID-19 deaths. In a tweet by Brian Wesbury, an economist, he reiterates the popular narrative around the idea that COVID-19 is only deadly for those with "comorbidities," (@wesbury, July 29, 2020) which is a consequential narrative for governmental regulations. While the tweet does not contain the term *scamdemic*, one of Twitter's top tweets in the search is a quote tweet by another user that includes his tweet and simply states, Scamdemic (@bradydawson16, July 29, 2020). Now, while this does not fall into the 500 or 1,000 retweet category, it's important to note that the Twitter search function does not calculate numbers for top search results, which is the default screen when a user searches terms or other criteria on the social media platform.

The overwhelming number of posts that included the term *scamdemic* in August 2020 centered around the misrepresentation of CDC data, as noted in the Wesbury tweet. In the United States, the country and most of its states were in full or partial lockdown mode during this time period. Tweets called out state governments and specifically their governors for these measures. For the tweets that had over 500 retweets, they contained two primary narratives: health-care workers who were resisting mask mandates and the implication that there were two systems of regulation going forth—ones for those in the elite class and ones for the rest of the population.

As the pandemic unfolds, the term begins to pop up as its own tweets rather than in reply to tweets. Candace Owens, who is a popular conservative commentator with over 3 million followers, posted a tweet on August 4, 2020, that called out the Washington, DC, mayor for exempting government employees from the mask mandate while requiring it of all others (@realcandaceO, August 4, 2020). This tweet is the first popular use of the term inside an "original" tweet with major followers. It has received, as of the writing of this essay, over 12,000 retweets, approximately 800 quote tweets, and 196 direct replies. While Owens did not include her source material, one can assume she is using a Breitbart article that was released the week prior to the tweet (Bleau 2020). A small group of respondents to her tweet included memes or responses that tied to the popular "Rules for Thee and not for me" rhetorical turn. While a small number of replies argued against her logic and stance, the preponderance of replies reiterated the scamdemic rhetoric by adding additional information such as website and video links or by adding to the narrative that COVID-19 regulations are fashioned ploys to restrict freedoms.

Late Winter and Early Spring 2021

On February 19, 2021, the term shows up in a tweet by @ZubyMusic, "I don't want to get roped into another rabbit hole regarding the scamdemic. . . .

But you've all been lied to and intentionally manipulated. I know it hurts, but it's true. Ready to stop playing this bizarre game of charades when everybody else is," which is retweeted approximately 750 times (@zubymusic, February 19, 2021). The tweet has hundreds of responses and responses to responses, demonstrating the complex network of conversation that may occur within the platform, and also adheres to a system of rumor and gossip, a kind of social grooming that Dunbar points to as a part of the work of gossip (Dunbar 1996). Zuby uses the second person in his tweet, an approach that attempts to group build, and adheres to Davison's model of persuasion and the third-person effect (Davison 1983, 3). So the combination of rumor/gossip structures with an approach that seeks to build rapport with an audience via the second person address begins to point to the types of false intimacies established via many social media platforms.

It is in the scamdemic hashtag and its popular rhetoric that readers can detect the foundation of the mask mandate resistance. The master narrative around mask mandates is a social class issue wherein Big Tech as well as the government and its employees are couched as other-than-citizens, or as one reply characterized it, the political class, while the rest of the population is living in a separate reality.

CASE STUDY: #PLANDEMIC/PLANDEMIC

Early Use and Initial Spread

In the late spring and summer of 2020, at the outset of the COVID-19 global pandemic, a controversial documentary series premiered called *Plandemic* (Willis 2020). The documentary added to a growing body of literature that has portrayed the spread of the coronavirus as a worldwide conspiracy planned and deployed by malevolent actors including people and organizations such as Dr. Anthony Fauci, Microsoft Founder and CEO Bill Gates, the World Health Organization, and various "mainstream media" outlets such as CNN, Google, NBC, and Facebook, to name a few. This popular literature saw and still sees the legislation, initiatives, and various governmental approaches to the detection, prevention, and treatment of the COVID-19 variants as a large-scale hoax meant to make people comply with a geo-political body or bodies that seek to destroy individual freedom and lead to some form of global slavery. Hellinger notes in his study of conspiracy theory in the context of the "Age of Trump" that one of the shared components in the disruptive nature of conspiracy is to "established order and hegemonic discourse" (Hellinger 2018, 98). Hellinger is among a long line of academics who examine the historical and contemporary place of conspiracy theory in U.S. political and popular culture. Bailyn (2017) pointed to a thread of conspiratorial thinking that infused the foundation of the United States in *The Ideological Origins of the American Revolution (1967)* which Hofstadter (1964) would pick up in "The Paranoid Style of American Politics." In his literary historiography of conspiracy theory in United States culture with its emphasis on the Revolution and Federalist eras, White (2002) notes that conspiracy theory acted in part as cultural analyses and institutional critique (26), which is an important note when thinking about this current analysis and how users are developing and deploying particular types of analyses through institutional critique that is leading to a grand narrative building in the form of conspiracy.

The term *plandemic* emerges once in the January 2020 Twitter feed, while in February 2020, the hashtag emerges in several tweets and the term gets tied to an offsite link to a February 15 video called "Wide Angle 2: Propaganda Plandemic with a Rothschild/Gates/Pilgrim Society Fingerprint." The video was viewed about 4,000 times before it was taken down from YouTube. In the video, the commenter with the username Ramola invokes several anti-Semitic organizations as her primary source materials including a site called Americans for Innovation and American Intelligence Media, which are mirror feeds, and Jon Rappaport's nomorefakenews.com, a site which focuses on the grand narrative of the Matrix as a real thing in the world (Ramola D Reports, 2020). This tweet and accompanying source material set a rhetorical frame and device for the ensuing hashtag communication arc. The plandemic is portrayed as an extension of a larger malevolent narrative, as intentional and calculated.

Unlike the scamdemic hashtag, which focuses early on the purported political maneuvering of bad actors who are taking advantage of the pandemic, the plandemic hashtag connects much earlier into the wider conspiracy theories popular among those who may be prone to follow such grand narratives and conspiracies put forward by QAnon or pre-QAnon stories involving sex trafficking or the new world order. I want to point out that while we see the edges of the QAnon conspiracies here, this is not about the QAnon phenomenon. This analysis focuses more on the landscape within which these avenues of communication happen and the distribution networks therein.

Summer 2020

In August 2020, just as with the scamdemic tag, the number of times the term *plandemic* is used increases exponentially. Concurrently, the second part of the documentary *Plandemic* was released in late July 2020, a release that did not garner the kind of attention and views the first part produced. Mike Rothschild, the author of *The Storm is Upon Us: How QAnon Became a Movement, Cult, and Conspiracy of Everything*, notes on August 19, 2020, that the failure of the sequel to the original documentary *Plandemic*, titled *Plandemic:*

Indoctrination, was in part due to social media platforms' enforcement of their community guidelines such as Facebook, which employed the restrictions to block access to the sequel, and Instagram and Tik Tok, which prevented the ability to share the video (Rothschild 2020). The video is online, most notably at alt-right sites such as Bitchute. Apart from the documentary, which may have aided in the popularity of the term, the hashtag and its accompanying term finds viability on the Twitter platform.

On August 19, 2020, an account (@dahboo7) tweeted out a clip from the documentary that highlighted the CDC's patent linked to the coronavirus, and while the tweet was retweeted fewer than 100 times, the account has a reach of over 40,000 followers. The tweet attached both the #scamdemic and #plandemic hashtags along with the hashtag #EXPOSED. The tweet reiterated the verbiage in the documentary clip, capitalizing on the hyperbolic nature of the all-caps to underline the notion of uncovering a grift. There were limited replies to the tweet, but all of them reinforced this narrative.

The account delivered on the documentarian's appeals to clip and share parts to wider audiences, a tactic that Ondrak (2020) examines as part of the spread of misinformation about COVID-19. This structure points to a memetic distribution of which the conspiracy network has taken special advantage, a type of spreadable media approach that gives audiences the power and authority to create content and distribute it in parts as well as to recreate that content through pastiche methods. Such authority impacts the public consumption of information, especially with regards to the plandemic tag.

Interestingly, tweets with the #plandemic hashtag also become adjacent to the release of Centers for Disease Control (CDC) information, which is a point of interest in the evolution of the tags—they become somewhat paratextual commentary on the release of authorized information as well as tweets from accounts with large (>10k) followers. For example, on August 19, 2020, two tweets provide material for examination of the paratextual nature of the hashtag. One exchange occurs via an account with a little over half a million followers, @catturd2, the feed for a daily podcast called "In the Litter Box." The account tweeted a conspiracy theory that implied the number of coronavirus cases would "explode" two weeks before the U.S. presidential election, to which a follower with approximately 5,000 followers replied with a Bill Gates meme that had him as a ventriloquist with Dr. Anthony Fauci as his dummy (@happykat9, August 29, 2020).

The original tweet was retweeted several thousand times, but the important note is that the respondent was replying to a well-known account, which begins to underscore the type of complex network involved in the spread and consumption of such information. This exchange demonstrates two key aspects of the plandemic rhetorical cycle—often it is in response to commentary on the virus spread and it employs a variety of communicative devices to invoke a pathos response, whether by grotesque humor in the form of memes or by emotional bids based on videos focused on crowds of anti-vaccination protestors.

On that same day, August 19, 2020, another tweet that tagged #plandemic was distributed by an account with more than 10,000 followers (@patriotjackib) that posted an article summarizing a Facebook Live Event where Dr. Anthony Fauci expressed his concern about relying on temperature checks as a way to contain the spread of the coronavirus (Meek 2020). The article link was captioned by the tweet author with "ARE YOU FREAKING KIDDING ME??? What is this #CovIDIOT going to change his mind about next? #Plandemic." Again, the use of capitalization is a rhetorical tactic, one of syntactical exaggeration; however, more important to note is the comment as an attachment to the emerging body of health-care advice, guidance, and guidelines, both as a piece of paratext and also as a demonstration of the continuing issues of scientific literacy that couches finding and applying new information as unreliable rather than as scientific methodology. Such documents and texts, from CDC press releases to interviews with official representatives, may be argued to act in the same way as authorized canon works and, in that authorization, the consistent need to annotate and comment on and against, allows for the reading of antifandom, a theme that will continue into the following year.

Late Winter and Early Spring 2021

The narrative of the outsider takes hold in the plandemic hashtag through highlighting the perceived contradictions between official guidelines and actions. In February 2021, much of the discourse in the hashtag centered on two themes: the push to reopen and the corruption at the heart of the perceived #plandemic, and in this time period we begin to see the globalization of this resistance. For example, in September 2020 the podcast/vodcast *Drink Champs* hosted the popular rapper Pitbull. During their conversation, the rapper proposed that the 2019 pandemic simulation hosted by Johns Hopkins University (Event 201) was a prefatory run for the COVID-19 pandemic. He offered an approximately three-minute interpretation of a series of events that led to the pandemic. His timeline included tying the simulation to work being done by the charity run by Microsoft CEO Bill Gates and his wife, Melinda Gates, and to a host of corporate head resignations as evidence of a planned operation behind the COVID-19 pandemic. His interpretation was widely disputed but the interesting note here is that while the podcast aired in September 2020, the plandemic hashtag was connected to this clip in February 2021 through a quote tweet from a user (@samanthamarika1) and then again by an account called @the_plandemic in June 2021, emphasizing a particular structure of distribution and citation on social media that looks for out of context sourcing.

One example comes in the form of a thread originating in a quote tweet, where a respondent can repost a tweet and caption it, which is structurally different from simply responding to a tweet. In this distribution, the tweeter assumes a type of source citation, to use the original tweet as an inspiration for commentary. One tweet, originally tweeted by @JamesMelville, does not contain the #plandemic tag; rather, the term is attached to the posted link and video by another user @queenvicstar, with the comment "Most probably the best tweet I've seen since the start of the plandemic" (February 20, 2021). Melville's tweet, which includes a two-minute video clip of him criticizing the British government's response to the COVID-19 crisis, calls for a return to "normality," and suggests that there are those who want to get back to living and those who want to be shielded. At no point did the original tweet imply a manipulated pandemic but the respondent, or quote tweeter, takes the opportunity to include Melville's pleas as part of this grand narrative building.

On February 20, 2021, approximately 100 tweets used the hashtag (not the term but the hashtag), and of those, a majority were either in response to other tweets or quote tweets, wherein the original post was from an official or verified account. For example, one Twitter user quote tweets Donald Trump Jr. who was linking Big Tech and algorithms to the perceived loss of free speech. (@donaldtrumpjr, February 20, 2021). The quote tweet is a string of hashtags including #freedomofspeech, #daretothink, #FarmersProtest, and #plandemic. What is interesting to note here is the connection to the #farmersprotest, which, as described in the introduction, has been an iconic representation of the resistance to COVID-19 policies and regulations, so there is a consistency in the symbolic language of these hashtags with one another, building a three dimensional or beyond the narrative that moves toward immersion due to its call for participation.

Summer 2021

In August 2021, the son of celebrity Tom Hanks, Chet Hanks (@chethanx), posted an Instagram video wherein he criticized vaccination mandates, which was tweeted out by an account with over 40,000 followers. That tweet included the hashtag #plandemic, drawing attention to the idea that the #plandemic is an analysis performed by free thinkers. At this point in time, in a search through the tweets on August 19, 2021, posts with the hashtag underscore a few themes: medical cynicism, as seen in a tweet from a South African account that proposes that the government wants to make "you" sick (@whitedisprin,

August 19, 2021); political opposition, such as when one Twitter user quote tweeted a large account (@maximebernier) that excerpted a clip of the World Health Organization meeting in August 2021 that spoke of "no return to the old normal" with tags #Covidiots, #freedoms, #votetrudeauout, #scamdemic, #plandemic, and #communismsucks; and a continuing frustration around the world with resounding critiques of governments in Australia, United Kingdom, Canada, India, South Africa, and the United States. The attached hashtags that emerge in August 2021 range from #endlockdown to #medicaltyranny.

In the summer 2021 we begin to see the culminating narrative around the plandemic tag, one that is a complicated series of assertions focused on corruption, malevolence, and grift. On August 19, 2021, a series of tweets emphasized the dangers to children from COVID-19 vaccines, the infringement of rights via vaccine passports, and again, the attachment of the tag to official CDC data on survival rates. The general call for noncompliance with public health and government guidelines saturate the tag, building a narrative of public distrust of institutions, but more importantly, how that mistrust has laid the groundwork for cynicism about the goals and objectives of public health experts.

OBSERVATIONS

Emergent Themes

The evolution of the hashtags across time demonstrates an intensifying and spreading narrative of mistrust in key public institutions. The rhetorical devices of humor and punnery add to the themes, yes, but also point toward a building *against* rather than building for, adopting many characteristics of the anti-fan. Additionally, the paratextual dependence of this conversation on *authorized information* dovetails with themes that are metafictive or metanarrative, and in this case, the hashtags tend to operate almost like notes on a text, if we adopt Genette's (1997) definition of note where it is "connected to a more or less definite segment of text and either placed opposite or keyed to this segment" (319). If the hashtags are paratextual meta notes or more postmodernish in their acts as gloss, then understanding the hashtags' evolutions must be attached to the increasing number of authorized texts and consequentially, authorized voices speaking about and around the pandemic, as a piece of their growth. I would argue this spread goes beyond a simple mechanical note, and rather the growth of these hashtags is much more akin to the idea of the correspondent or addressed note, wherein there is a perceived audience to which these tags are appealing.

While some themes diverged in the tags, with one tag more and more focused on economic disadvantages and the other focused on intentional and malevolent deterioration of rights and liberties, both tags shared similar themes. From the narrative building, three choruses emerge as keystone skepticisms: technophobia (or more accurately, technodemia—more terror and dread than fear), parental rights, and medical cynicism.

Technodemia

As we can gather from the selected tweets, one strong thread of the grand narrative building involves the suspicion about and fear of big tech's place in the global marketplace. Such a narrative is not new but the theme of it saturates the hashtag, pointing fingers at the tech industry as everything from producers of ill-conceived vaccines to censorship hubs such as in the Donald J. Trump Jr. tweet where he calls out social media companies for infringement of free speech. While posters did not recognize the irony of lobbing such criticisms on the very platforms they were criticizing, the point of dread still stands. Such technophobia is more technodemia or dread, rather than fear. As noted in the Pitbull example, there is a large audience who perceives technology as a tool for enslavement, as the global population inhabiting a kind of science-fiction-like landscape where big tech plays the villain.

This dread or terror is demonstrated quite pointedly in the use of Bill Gates as the icon of technological malevolence. Gates's celebrity as a big tech entrepreneur coincides with the public work his charities have been involved in for a decade or more, but his connection to Jeffrey Epstein has enabled the continued accusations against him such as seen in one August 2020 tweet that says "covid is planned and bill gates is a pedo #saveourchildren" (@basedcum, August 21, 2020). The correlation between big tech terror and the rhetoric surrounding the imagined, endangered child helps to fuel the parental rights approach that many anti-vaccination and COVID-19 conspiracy theorists have adopted as a banner movement.

Parental Rights

Instead of civil or human rights, many of the examined threads started to gather around the ideas of parental rights, especially in terms of the children affected by the pandemic. The most potent example of this movement was the thread around the supposed taking of the children from parents who refused to adhere to the governmental restrictions. The move toward parental rights ties into other high-level conspiracy theories such as the fears around grooming, pedophilia, and sex trafficking, to name a few. The invocation of the parental rights angle is what I would argue is the most apparent performance of antifandom against governmental regulation as well as against technological progression. It is a pathos call to action that makes it difficult, almost impossible, to argue against, and in the ever-changing landscape of reproductive technologies, the call to a traditional parent/child bond is especially potent. As Hall (1999) argues in "The Origins of Parental Rights," we have moved from an Enlightenment-era concept of parent as owner of labor to parent as owner of genetic material (79). So parental rights appeal to an audience who are concerned with governmental intrusion into the traditional nuclear family conceit.

This theme has a real-world consequence and ramification as the debate surrounding parental rights moves into school board meetings, state legislative chambers, and across governors' desks as new laws, especially in conservative states such as Iowa, Indiana, Florida, Texas, and Georgia.

Medical Cynicism

Besides the terror over technology and the entreaties to parental rights, the most striking and perhaps consistent theme found throughout the hashtags, both plandemic and scamdemic, pointed to an active distrust in public health institutions, both as protectors of the public and credible sources of information. The cynicism surrounding the motives and desires of public health entities has become the canon of source material around which much of this grand narrative takes place. Data releases, guidelines, and other authorized forms of distributed information were treated much like an episode of a television show—material for critical fodder and for story building beyond the press and information releases.

The Chet Hanks example gives a glimpse into that resistance to public health authority. As the pandemic unfolded, more and more participants in the tags couched the data and press releases from various public health institutions as guided by either greed or malice, as either arbitrary or incompetent. Scientific literacy—a literacy which values not only scientific knowledge but also the process that values methodology, observation, and the changes that emerge from reiteration—disappears behind the need for absolutes. Like Bill Gates, Dr. Anthony Fauci has become an iconic representation for those who wish to rally against public health information and regulations. When Fauci suggested that young children continue to mask, one poster with approximately 10,000 followers tweeted with a link to a Federalist article,

> This is so incredibly concerning. Fauci cites no actual evidence, places unmasking kids as a "hope" and then punts to the @CDCgov who have proven themselves to be incompetent partisan hacks in the pocket of the Teacher's unions. This is a war on children and parents. (@e_got_tweets, August 9, 2021)

In this one August 9, 2021 tweet, the issues of parental rights and medical cynicism blend as one critique.

There is much more to be learned from these threads. As waves of COVID-19 continue to ebb and flow and the volatile debates around masking, vaccination, and public health behaviors become progressively disruptive, the possibility of an ever greater division between what is information and what is misinformation increases.

CONCLUSION

When I began this inquiry, the question most pressing on my mind was simple: How does one believe _____ about the pandemic? The blank included ideas such as QAnon, global political conspiracy, and that malicious and ill-intentioned governmental and corporate leaders are creating and shaping a worldwide pandemic to enslave millions. I asked these questions in a somewhat arrogant way, pretending an outrage that has since turned into part sadness, part horror, and part shame. I admit to my fault of arrogance now as I compile and share this writing. What started as an interrogation of two hashtags, #scamdemic and #plandemic, morphed away from a didactic discussion of social media and misinformation into a reflective work on meaning-making and community building. While some of the content felt like an assault on my senses at times, and I have tried hard not to repeat that mistake for my readers, what I ended up learning from this project was much more about the ways in which digital isolation works, what falling into a void of information might look like, and how the public trust in institutions has fractured so badly that recovery may be next to impossible, and, to a degree, the institution of education, both higher and secondary, has complied with these moves. This essay is in part journey, in part investigation, and in part a call to action.

The work of unspooling the threads connecting COVID-19 information, misinformation, and conspiracy is a project of layers and nuance. For example, one clear thread that becomes apparent throughout the hashtags is the juxtaposition of cynicism regarding media and government with the exceptional outsider narrative, in the work of studying and reporting on what appear to be fringe groups but who have taken a kind of central attention point in the public discourse around disease prevention and treatment. This is not the place to judge them but rather to reflect on how institutions bear some responsibility for this outcome.

While I took time to examine rhetorical devices, wordplay and choice, I also began to detect a particular narrative that highlights the disintegration of public trust in governmental institutions from health care to education, a disintegration that reveals the failures of those institutions to aptly communicate with a disenfranchised public, and how that disenfranchisement opens the portal to meaning-making devices that couch transparency as conspiracy, scientific method as unreliable narration, and regulation as enslavement. These rhetorical moves are not new but the collision of a public health crisis with an increasingly unregulated and apparently (but not really) democratized social media landscape provides an opportunity to see how misinformation evolves into a set of interpretations and assertions that have a real and tangible impact on all of us. The structures of the COVID-19 misinformation loop have had devastating consequences for the world, but these structures are not inherently new to the pandemic. Rather, the structures of misinformation go beyond mere profitability for some bad actors to the heart of how certain groups choose to make meaning. Much of the misinformation in the hashtags cast a catastrophic narrative of scientific skepticism, political disenfranchisement, and affective caricatures that get performed through transcendental stories of corruption, greed, and worldwide conspiracy.

REFERENCES

Bailyn, Bernard. 2017. *The Ideological Origins of the American Revolution.* 50th anniversary ed. Cambridge: Harvard University Press.

Bal, Mieke. 1994. *On Meaning-Making: Essays in Semiotics.* Leni, UT: Polebridge Press.

Bleau, Hannah. 2020. "DC Mask Mandate Exempts Lawmakers and Government Employees." *Breitbart Report,* July 27, 2020. www.breitbart.com/politics/2020/07/23/dc-mask-mandate-exempts-lawmakers-government-employees.

Davison, W. Phillips. 1983. "The Third Person Effect in Communication." *The Public Opinion Quarterly* 47, no. 1 (Spring): 1–15.

Dawkins, Richard. 1976. *The Selfish Gene.* New York: Oxford University Press.

Dunbar, Robin. 1996. *Grooming, Gossip, and the Evolution of Language.* Cambridge: Harvard University Press.

Ford, Sam, Henry Jenkins, and Joshua Green. 2013. *Spreadable Media: Creating Value and Meaning in a Networked Culture.* New York: New York University Press.

Gal, Noam. 2019. "Ironic Humor on Social Media as Participatory Boundary Work." *New Media & Society* 21, no. 3 (October): 729–49.

Genette, Gerard. 1997. *Paratexts: Thresholds of Interpretations.* Translated by Jane E. Lewin. New York: Cambridge University Press.

Giappone, Krista Bonello Rutter. 2015. "Self-Reflexivity and Humor in Adventure Games." *Game Studies* 15, no. 1 (July). http://gamestudies.org/1501/articles/bonello_k.

Goffman, Erving. 2021. *The Presentation of Self in Everyday Life.* 3rd ed. New York: Anchor Press.

Gray, Jonathan. 2005. "Antifandom and the Moral Text." *American Behavioral Scientist* 48, no. 7 (March): 840–58.

———. 2019. "How Do I Dislike Thee? Let Me Count the Ways." In *Antifandom: Dislike and Hate in the Digital Age,* edited by Melissa Click, 25–41. New York: New York University Press.
Hall, Barbara. 1999. "The Origins of Parental Rights." *Public Affairs Quarterly* 13, no. 1 (January): 73–82.
Hellinger, Daniel. 2018. *Conspiracies and Conspiracy Theories in the Age of Trump.* Cham, Switzerland: Palgrave Macmillan.
Hofstadter, Richard. 1964. "The Paranoid Style in American Politics." *Harper's* (November): 77–86.
Jenkins, Henry. 2006. *Convergence Culture.* New York: New York University Press.
Lyotard, Jean Francois. 1989. *The Postmodern Condition: A Report on Knowledge.* Translated by Geoff Bennington and Brian Massumi. Minneapolis, MN: University of Minnesota Press.
Meek, Andy. 2020. "Dr. Fauci Explains Why Temperature Checks to Fight COVID-19 Are Pointless." August 18. https://bgr.com/science/temperature-checks-too-inaccurate-to-fight-coronavirus-fauci-interview.
Ondrak, Jon. 2020. "Plandemic 2: Memetic Boogaloo." *Logically,* August 19. www.logically.ai/articles/plandemic-2-memetic-boogaloo.
Pruitt-Young, Sharon. 2022. "A Canadian Judge Has Frozen Access to Donations for the Trucker Convoy Protest." *NPR,* February 10, 2022. www.npr.org/2022/02/10/1080022827/a-canadian-judge-has-frozen-access-to-donations-for-the-trucker-convoy-protest.
Ramola D. Reports. 2020. "Wide Angle 2: Propaganda Plandemic with a Rothschild/Gates/Pilgrim Society Fingerprint." AltCensored. Video, 1:08:53. https://altcensored.com/watch?v=dFmcrlafx-o.
Rose, Margaret. 1993. *Parody: Ancient, Modern, and Post-Modern.* New York: Cambridge University Press.
Rothschild, Mike. 2020. "Why the Sequel to a Massive Coronavirus Conspiracy Movie Completely Flopped." *The Daily Dot,* August 19. www.dailydot.com/debug/plandemic-2-indoctornation-conspiracy-theories.
Sanchez-Paramo, Carolina. 2020. "COVID-19 Will Hit the Poor Hardest. Here's What We Can Do about It." *World Bank,* April 23. https://blogs.worldbank.org/voices/covid-19-will-hit-poor-hardest-heres-what-we-can-do-about-it.
Sandvoss, Cornel. 2019. "The Politics of Against: Political Participation, Anti-Fandom, and Populism." In *Antifandom: Dislike and Hate in the Digital Age,* edited by Melissa Click, 125–46. New York: New York University Press.
Sunstein, Cass. 2014. *On Rumors: How Falsehood Spread, Why We Believe Them and What Can Be Done.* Princeton, NJ: Princeton University Press.
White, Ed. 2002. "The Value of Conspiracy Theory." *American Literary History* 14, no. 1 (Spring): 1–31.
Willis, Mikki, director. 2020. *Plandemic.* Elevate Films.

Chapter 3

Social Media, COVID-19, Misinformation, and Ethics

A Descriptive Study of American Adults' Perceptions

Tammy Swenson-Lepper and Heidi J. Hanson

Since the beginning of the COVID-19 pandemic, numerous hoaxes about the virus and its vaccine have been widely shared on social media, including YouTube videos stating that the vaccine includes a microchip that allows people to be controlled by the government or large corporations (Bond 2020), that 5G mobile phone service is causing the virus, that vaccines cause autism (Bond 2021), that the vaccine "will alter people's DNA" (Ramjug 2021), and that ivermectin is a treatment for COVID-19 (Alba 2021), among many others.[1]

While misinformation and fake news on social media may seem like a minor player in the fight again the COVID-19 pandemic, Ognyanova et al. (2021) found that "belief in vaccine misinformation is associated with lower vaccination rates and higher vaccine resistance" (4). A study by the de Beaumont Foundation (2021) found that people who "said social media was an influential source were *16 percent less likely* to report that they had received at least one dose of the COVID-19 vaccine" (emphasis in original). They were "far more likely to believe false information about vaccines." Research has shown that people who are politically conservative tend to believe conspiracy theories about the COVID-19 vaccine and are, therefore, less likely to be vaccinated (Ognyanova et al. 2021). This means that the red states of the South, Midwest, and West are more likely to have greater numbers of unvaccinated people. According to Wood (2021), residents of "the reddest tenth of

---

[1] Special thanks to Susan Byom, librarian in charge of Interlibrary Loan at Winona State University, without whom this chapter would not have been possible.

the country saw death rates that were six times higher than the bluest tenth" in the month of October 2021.

Misinformation about COVID-19, masking, and vaccines on social media has thus had a major effect on the spread of COVID-19 in the United States. However, little work has been done to examine how the general public views the ethicality of posts on social media about these topics. People have been asked to state their beliefs about the legal consequences that social media platforms should face for sharing misinformation or fake news (Jang and Kim 2018). Some people believe that misinformation should not be flagged because they believe it is censorship, while others believe that all misinformation should be flagged or removed from social media platforms. The reasons why people believe that information should be flagged or left alone are most likely part of people's value systems or perspectives on what is right or wrong, thus making it an ethical issue.

Investigating fake news and misinformation on social media is of significance in the current news situation of the United States. Slightly more than 80 percent of Americans use YouTube, while about 70 percent of adult Americans use Facebook (Auxier and Anderson 2021). Additionally, the majority of social media users say that they "visit these platforms [Facebook, Snapchat, and Instagram] on a daily basis" (Auxier and Anderson 2021). Most U.S. residents are getting at least some of their news from a digital device, and almost 51 percent sometimes or often get their news from social media (Matsa and Naseer 2021). Younger adults (ages 18–29) are most likely to get their news from social media (71%), with older adults (ages 30–49, 50–64) tending to get their digital news from news websites or apps (Matsa and Naseer 2021).

In the literature review of this project, we will discuss misinformation and fake news, psychological and demographic factors that contribute to belief in misinformation, the Third-Person Effect, methods for fighting misinformation, and perceptions of ethics in social media more generally.

LITERATURE REVIEW

Misinformation and Fake News

Since COVID-19 news started to spread in early 2020, people have become anxious because of exaggerated and "suspenseful headlines" regarding the pandemic. Consistent exposure to exaggerated information has many consequences for average news consumers (Bratu 2020). Various claims and narratives regarding COVID-19 have been spread on various forms of media, including written news, headline news, radio news, social media, and so on (Gerosa et al. 2021). Distinct factors affect a person's susceptibility to these claims and the chances of the average person spreading them intentionally or unintentionally.

There are a variety of fake news claims that have circulated in the media since the beginning of the COVID-19 pandemic. One popular piece of misinformation that spread in multiple countries about the COVID-19 virus is that 5G technology caused the pandemic (Bruns, Harrington and Hurcombe 2020). According to Bruns, Harrington, and Hurcombe (2020), rumors circulated in countries such as Romania and China that the COVID-19 vaccine was deadly and would be activated by 5G radiation; another rumor circulated in the UK that stated 5G technology "destroys oxygen." Claims regarding 5G technology led consumers to believe that COVID-19 is a fraud, which causes behavioral and attitudinal changes. According to Germani and Biller-Andorno (2021), anti-vaccination claims and misinformation were spread on social media by former president Donald Trump; Trump's high profile caused more extensive belief in the fear-inducing claim that vaccines are associated with autism.

The concept of disinformation is important in understanding differing intentions social media users have when spreading information. Liu and Huang (2020) describe disinformation as "false or misleading information that is spread deliberately to deceive the public" (789). One reason people may intentionally mislead the public by spreading disinformation is the concept of freedom of speech. In a study done by Ardèvol-Abreu, Delponti, and Rodríguez-Wangüemert (2020) some people "appealed to their freedom of speech and argued that they may share the fake content just because they 'agree' with it 'even if the speech is wrong'" (789). Atehortua and Patino (2021) suggest that extremist movements have taken advantage of the pandemic to spread hateful messages, some affiliated with anti-vaccination strategies. The 5G claims made on social media appear to be a product of conspiracist beliefs from before the pandemic; these beliefs led to suspicions of many others, including people from China and global elites (Bruns, Harrington and Hurcombe 2020). Bruns, Harrington, and Hurcombe (2020) also state that, in general, conspiracy theories, specifically on Facebook, are spread to exploit the fears of users and push "conspiracist narratives" so that the posts will be shared more often.

But what if the sharing of misinformation is unintentional? According to Apukea and Omara (2021), altruistic people, who they define as those who "enjoy the act of helping others" are more likely to unintentionally share misinformation. Altruistic people who do not pay close attention to the information they are sharing may share the information in hopes of making a positive impact. Altruism is known to be a cultural trait in the country of Nigeria, where the dissemination of fake news and misinformation has been shown to be a prevailing issue (Apukea and Omara 2021). Many people spread misinformation because they do not pay close attention to the original source of the information being shared (Ardèvol-Abreu, Delponti and Rodríguez-Wangüemert 2020). Ardèvol-Abreu, Delponti, and Rodríguez-Wangüemert (2020) ran a study that found that warning labels made by social media platforms on misinformation or fake news merely stand as "one more piece of information to consider" to social media users, rather than a reason to stop or reconsider sharing (5). They also found that many social media users believe that "truth is provisional" in terms of COVID-19, which they explain as believing "something that is found to be false today might be true tomorrow" (8). Not putting in the time to fact-check information and to make sure it comes from trustworthy sources perpetuates the spread of misinformation.

Whether people spread misinformation intentionally or unintentionally, a sizable percentage of the population has believed claims such as the 5G conspiracy theory (Tiffany 2020). General mistrust of the government is a factor in believing misinformation and fake news; for example, Greene and Murphy (2020) found that government warnings against misinformation did not impact the behavior of social media users and did not decrease the impacts of fake news exposure. Some social media users and other individuals tend to believe the government is hiding or fabricating key information regarding the COVID-19 pandemic (Quinn, Fazel and Peters 2021). Emotional intelligence is a factor in the susceptibility to fake news. Preston et al. (2021) found a significant positive correlation between fake news detection and high emotional intelligence test scores. In another study, a higher education level was positively correlated to general knowledge, which can assist in fake news detection (although the fake news beliefs cannot be predicted) (Gerosa et al. 2021). However, other factors such as age, sex, and race do not appear to play a part in fake news detection (Abraham and Mandalaparthy 2021; Wright and Duong 2021). Overall, fake news is widely spread both intentionally and unintentionally (Atehortua and Patino 2021). Thus, the dissemination of fake news overwhelms trustworthy news sources, which leads to greater levels of public confusion and "counterproductive reduction of COVID-19 transmissions" (Bratu 2020, 129).

Because of the easy access to fake news and misinformation, individuals with poor mental health may resort to "compulsive pursuance of COVID-19 information to reduce their anxiety" (Bratu 2020, 129). This media-fueled trauma affected healthcare facilities already swamped by a large volume of COVID-19 patients. Bratu (2020) found that in addition to people unnecessarily traveling to healthcare facilities because of their fears about COVID-19 (fears stoked by fake news), people also resorted to panic buying essential items because media platforms reported the undersupply of resources (129). Since the onset of the pandemic took place in China, xenophobia has risen in the United States (Wright and Duong 2021). They found that being white was associated with higher levels of xenophobia caused by fake news regarding COVID-19.

Fake news dissemination also contributes to increasing anti-vaccination efforts; claims mentioning microchips, autism, and so on have increased public condemnation of vaccine use. Anti-vaccination communities on Twitter had very few original posts but significantly higher numbers of retweets, in comparison to the pro-vaccination pages with higher amounts of original content but lower retweet numbers. They found that anti-vaccination communities on Twitter act as echo chambers of misinformation and disinformation, where the users share common beliefs and attitudes with a smaller number of profiles. This also contributes to the polarization of the vaccine debate, which can sway the hesitant into believing misinformation about vaccines and reducing the vaccination rates (Germani and Biller-Andorno 2021).

Finally, the dissemination of fake news and misinformation creates a cycle of misinformation on social media platforms. Many social media platforms have an algorithm that presents posts based on what a user has liked and interacted with before; with the polarization of social media feeds, counter-arguments and factual information may not be seen by people who interact with misinformation often (Germani and Biller-Andorno 2021, 9). Ironically, content removals and bans, rather than decreasing the spread of misinformation, have the unintended impact of "strengthening the beliefs of conspiracy theorists for whom such interventions are proof that they are in the process of uncovering deeper secrets that the establishment does not want them to see" (Bruns, Harrington and Hurcombe 2020, 26). The cycle of misinformation perpetuates itself through public confusion and the attempts to decrease the impact of fake news on the public, which makes solutions difficult to find.

Psychological and Demographic Characteristics

Many psychological factors contribute to the viewing, understanding, and spreading of fake news. Political viewpoints can increase bias, thus increasing incivility in social media users; this can also reduce the effectiveness of mitigation strategies regarding COVID-19 transmission. Bumsoo (2020) states that incivility occurred in multiple forms, including name calling, aspersions, vulgarity, and pejorative speech, which all depend on the audience for the comments. Individuals with larger network sizes, specifically on Twitter, are less likely to use uncivil language. He explains that individuals with smaller social media networks may have less of an opportunity to understand viewpoints different from their own. Bumsoo (2020) also states that partisan media encourages the use of uncivil language, especially during political elections (524).

When viewing news regarding COVID-19, Calvillo et al.(2020) found that conservative participants were significantly more likely to perceive themselves as less vulnerable to the risks of the COVID-19 virus. The polarization of news shapes the way that news consumers perceive it, as conservatives seem to be less accurate in discerning between real and fake news (Calvillo et al. 2020). Lawson and Kakkar (2021) found that low-conscientiousness conservatives have a greater desire for chaos than liberals and are more likely to share fake news.

Confirmation bias, along with other biases, also play a role in the sharing and understanding of fake news. Westerwick, Johnson, and Knobloch-Westerwick (2017) define confirmation bias as "the phenomenon that individuals select messages more frequently that align with preexisting opinions over information that challenges preexisting views." This, partnered with selective exposure, which "denotes that individuals selectively attend to messages they can choose from and do not spend equal time with all available messages" (343), led to the conclusion that participants in this study "favored attitude-consistent content over attitude-challenging content," meaning they agreed with information that aligned with their existing opinions (359). However, individuals with different information processing systems may respond in diverse ways, and selective exposure may impact them differently in terms of political messages (359). Van der Meer, Hameleers, and Kroon (2020) have found that confirmation, source, and negativity bias all have significant roles in selective exposure, but confirmation bias is the main factor in determining an individual's selective exposure. Ven der Meer, Hameleers, and Kroon (2020) define source bias as "when people show a tendency to avoid engaging in repeated active news selection" (938) and explains that negativity bias is the idea that "audiences might exhibit a (unconscious) preference for negative over positive political news" (939). They also note that individuals who are more skeptical and less critical of the news they consume are more likely to foster polarized divides in their views on specified issues, such as COVID-19 (957).

Fake news on social media can affect the behaviors of social media users; COVID-19 conspiracy theories may indirectly influence individuals' compliance with the best mitigation practices that prevent COVID-19 (Vitriol and Marsh 2021). More specifically, positive perceptions and beliefs regarding scientific statements were related to increased mitigation behaviors regarding the pandemic (Vitriol and Marsh 2020, 7). When people are more influenced by qualified, high-quality information, the total infection rate is likely to go down. Because individuals commonly rely on their peers' health statuses to infer infection risk, this can lead to them being unaware of the actual risk they are facing during the pandemic. For example, if an individual's neighbor does not have COVID-19, the individual may base their perception of the overall infection rate on their neighbor's health status (Du et al. 2021). Du et al. also state that the total infection rates may go down when people view high-quality social media posts because high-quality posts increase awareness of disease risk and promote behaviors that mitigate the spread of disease.

However, using social media as the prime source of news tends to be detrimental to not only understanding the risks of COVID-19 and effective mitigation behaviors, but also increases the intake and belief in fake news and conspiracy theories. Individuals who trust news from social media are more likely to believe in COVID-19 fake news and conspiracies; those with a higher education who trust governmental information sources are less likely to believe COVID-19 fake news and myths (Melki et al. 2021). Stecula and Pickup (2021) have found that using Facebook and YouTube for news makes individuals with low cognitive reflection levels more likely to believe conspiracies. Stecula and Pickup (2021) state that it is those who succumb to gut reactions who are significantly more likely to believe in conspiracy theories, while those with high cognitive reflection levels, who can slow down and resist the incorrect intuitive answers, are unaffected by Facebook use and are less likely to endorse conspiracies. The majority of individuals on social media believe sources such as doctors, medical practitioners, and other competent people are trustworthy (Tayal and Bharathi 2021). Tayal and Bharathi also found that people are more likely to share information they have fact-checked, but people rarely fact or cross-check the information they find on social media with other news sources.

Third-Person Effect

Davison began the study of Third-Person Effect in 1983. He defined Third-Person Effect as "people will tend to overestimate the influence that mass communications have on the attitudes and behaviors of others" (3). Perloff (1999) defines it more comprehensively and says that the Third-Person Effect

> is the belief that communications exert a stronger impact on others than on the self.... A key assumption of the TPE [Third-Person Effect] is that perceptions of media effects on the self and others are distinct entities, that is, individuals can and do separate out in their minds perceptions on communication effects on others and the self. (355)

Thus, people assume that mass communication affects other people's beliefs, attitudes, and behaviors, but not their own. Over the intervening years since these original papers were written, scholars published dozens of studies about the Third-Person Effect, examining areas related to advertising (Xie 2016), disasters (Wei et al. 2015), the influence of poll results on opinions (F. L. Lee

2010), political participation (Banning 2006), television violence (Salwen and Dupagne 2001) and many more. In this review of literature, we will focus on select studies related to Third-Person Effect and misinformation, social media, and health information, including COVID-19. This chapter primarily focuses on misinformation in online sources, especially social media.

There are two types of misinformation in online sources: fake news and general misinformation. Fake news is misinformation that is designed to look like it was produced by a news organization, can be proven untrue, and the mistruths are designed to influence people with specific persuasive intents, be they to sell you a product, candidate, or political perspective (Baek, Kang, and Kim 2019, Hwang and Kwon 2017). Misinformation, on the other hand, is still intentionally false, but the information is not presented as being created by a news organization (Liu and Huang 2020). Liu and Huang (2020) found that "fake news exposure on social media . . . is linked to the perception of disinformation effects on close others, but not on distant others" (792), meaning that individuals don't believe that they are susceptible to misinformation, but they believe that their close friends and family members are; they also believe that distant others are even more susceptible to misinformation (Ștefăniță, Corbu and Buturoiu 2018). Thus, as in previous Third-Person Effect work, individuals do not feel personally susceptible to lies about COVID-19 online, but believe others are susceptible to them.

In general, people believe that they are better at assessing misinformation than their peers, but they are more likely to believe that they are better at it than those who are close to them if they have greater education, are more interested in politics, and have greater levels of confirmation bias, "which translates into people being more confident about being able to quickly understand and evaluate a situation" (Corbu et al. 2020, 171). They also found that "less Facebook dependent, higher educated people, who are more interested in politics, estimating to encounter misleading information more often are more affected by third person perceptions about the ability to detect fake news" (Corbu et al. 2020, 173–174) Thus, people with more education who reported not using Facebook very often strongly believed that others would believe fake news and misinformation much more than they would. As Corbu et al. point out, this makes social media users believe that they are less likely to be misled by fake news than their friends, family, and distant others (173–74).

Political affiliation also ties into the Third-Person Effect for people's perceptions of others' ability to evaluate fake news and misinformation, especially in relation to the 2016 election. Given the strength of the partisan divides that still exist, it is likely that the findings that follow are still relevant and relate to COVID-19. Jang and Kim (2018) have found that Democrats are more likely to believe Republicans are susceptible, while Republicans believe Democrats are more susceptible, thus making the divide between members of the political parties even greater. As they point out, "American voters are more likely to think that they are smarter than others and that they are not easily influenced by false attempts at persuasion" (299).

In the past decade or so, scholars have started studying the third-person effect as it relates to social media use. In their survey of people who primarily get their news from social media, Yang and Horning (2020) found that participants believed others were more affected by fake news than they were. Further, they found that "the more individuals perceived that fake news influenced others, the more they thought fake news was socially undesirable" (6); counterintuitively, they were also less likely to approve of censoring news that was fake. Tsay-Vogel (2016) found that people believe others used Facebook for longer periods of time and more intensively than they did (1965). Schweisberger, Billinson and Chock (2014), using experimental methods, learned that users believed that low relevance stories affected others more than themselves, but that higher impact stories affected the users more. This study is of particular note because it examined stories presented on social media or the internet that were of high or low relevance to the participants. The more relevant the story, the more likely participants were to believe it had more of an effect on them than on others. People tend to believe that others are more susceptible to fake news than they are, but they do not want fake news censored. Yang and Horning (2020) propose people oppose governmental censorship for a variety of reasons, including a free press or not having a clear understanding of what fake news is (7).

Consistent with previous research, the Third-Person Effect occurs when users interact with information about health information (Stavrositu and Kim 2014), pandemic flu (not COVID-19) (Lee and Park 2016), and COVID-19 on social media (Yang and Tian 2021). Stavrositu and Kim (2014) found typical results when they showed participants information about cancer that had low metrics (few shares and likes); people believed others would be more influenced than the participants, but when the metrics were high (lots of shares and likes) the Third-Person Effect was not significant, suggesting that likes and shares are perceived to influence both the self and others (65). Lee and Park (2016) used an experimental design to examine participants' responses to cable news stories about the H1N1 flu, controlling for the story's presentation of the severity of the pandemic, how able participants were to prevent the illness (efficacy), and the credibility of the source. Their results showed typical Third-Person Effect findings, in that participants believed others would be more affected by the messages than they were. The Third-Person Effect was related to the participants' willingness to be vaccinated; the greater the Third-Person Effect, the less likely they were to consider getting vaccinated against the H1N1 influenza virus. When the virus was perceived as severe and there were effective ways to control its spread, the message from the media was perceived as having more effect on the self. Yang and Tian (2021) have found, as did Corbu et al. (2020), that participants believe their friends and family are susceptible to fake news about COVID-19, but that those that are socially more distant are even more susceptible to fake news and that the fake news would change both their thoughts and behaviors.

Fighting Misinformation on Social Media

Misinformation is rife on social media, especially in the context of the COVID-19 pandemic. Some scholars have researched the best ways to combat misinformation and found mixed results. Pennycook et al. (2020) found that a "nudge" toward accuracy or truth by reminding them to think about accuracy led to less willingness to share false headlines, while replication of the study by Roozenbeek, Freeman, and van der Linden (2021) found a much smaller effect. Roozenbeek, Freeman, and van der Linden (2021) almost doubled their sample size for their second round of data collection because their first round of data collection showed no effect from a "nudge" toward the truth (1174). When people are like those they follow or interact with on social media (homophily), they are less likely to fact-check what others are posting; "users were more careful by fact checking COVID-19 related news on [social media] when they were in less homophilous [social media] environments and generally aware of the circulation of COVID-19 fake news on [social media]" (Schuetz, Sykes, and Venkatesh 2021, 382).

Perceptions of Ethics in Social Media

Since social media became a major force in people's lives, the key ethical issues that scholars have studied have dealt with issues where individual users affect other individuals most directly, like cyberbullying, trolling, and stalking (Swenson-Lepper and Kerby 2019). Social media users also consider privacy a significant concern, but often they are concerned about how organizations with which they are affiliated might use their data, either their university or their workplace (Drouin et al. 2015, O'Connor, Schmidt, and Drouin 2016). Since the publication of our article in 2019 (Swenson-Lepper and Kerby 2019), little quantitative work has been done on social media users' perceptions of ethical issues in social media use; a search of the EBSCO databases for the term "social media" and "ethics" or "normativity" in scholarly articles found very few new articles have been published in recent years. The articles we found are discussed below.

Current research in ethics and social media tends to fall into multiple categories; research on professional standards and discussion of ethical standards for using social media as a research tool is among the most discussed. For instance, articles have been written about how nurses (Grace 2021), therapists (Wu and Sonne 2021), social workers (Cartwright 2017), and meteorologists (Mulvey, Deleon, and Sowder 2020) use or should use social media. Scholars are also concerned with using social media as a research tool and have worked to create ethical guidelines for research in a variety of fields, including public health (Hunter et al. 2018), human subjects research (Hokke et al. 2020), and bioethics (Rattani and Johns 2017).

A small amount of research has been conducted specifically on how users view the ethicality of behavior on social media. For instance, a study of nurses used hypothetical cases to examine nurses' evaluations of "ethical violations to hypothetical case studies involving social media use" (Demiray et al. 2020, 84). They found that more highly educated nurses were more able to perceive ethical issues in some of the cases with which they were presented. Michaelidou and Micevski (2019) examined consumers' perceptions of the use of social media analytics by organizations and found that consumers are less concerned about ethical issues like privacy when they perceive the organization to be trustworthy. Berriman and Thomson (2015) did in-depth interviews with nine teenagers to examine their views of how they manage ethical issues they face online and found that the teens are concerned about risking privacy and experiencing trolling, among other issues. Bagdasaraov et al. (2017) found that undergraduate students with more exposure to ethical issues in social media were more likely to be able to identify ethical issues in the scenarios about social media in a survey, even when the original ethical issues participants were exposed to were not identified. They posit "that ethical norms, though not described in our scale or probed about directly, may have driven participants to connect the themes and transfer to the scenarios presented in our study" (557). Thus, most current studies have not asked participants to identify ethical issues in social media, but instead have placed ethical issues identified by the researchers in front of participants.

Research Questions

Based on our previous research about communication ethics and social media (Swenson-Lepper 2011, Swenson-Lepper, and Kerby 2019), we wanted to know what people believe to be the greatest ethical issues or most unethical social media posts related to the COVID-19 virus, vaccines, and masking on social media. Some of these issues are likely tied to freedom of speech (Ardèvol-Abreu, Delponti, and Rodríguez-Wangüemert 2020) and misinformation or fake news itself (Germani and Biller-Andorno 2021).

> RQ1a: What do participants believe to be the greatest ethical issue related to the COVID-19 virus, vaccine, or masking on social media?

RQ1b: What do participants believe are the most unethical ways that they have seen social media used related to the COVID-19 virus, vaccine, or masking?

While scholars have found that some people share misinformation because they are altruistic (Apukea and Omara 2021) or because they do not closely check sources (Ardèvol-Abreu, Delponti and Rodríguez-Wangüemert 2020), we wanted to know whether people will acknowledge that they have shared false information. Based on research about the Third-Person Effect (Ștefăniță, Corbu and Buturoiu 2018), we thought that respondents might believe that their friends and family have shared false information about COVID-related topics. This leads to two research questions and a hypothesis.

RQ2a: Do participants believe that they have shared false information about the COVID-19 virus, vaccine, or masking?

RQ2b: Do participants believe that they or their friends and family have shared false information about the COVID-19 virus, vaccine, or masking?

H1: Based on the Third-Person Effect, participants will believe that their friends and family members have shared more false information about the COVID-19 virus, vaccine, or masking than they have.

In general, recent research shows that conservatives are more likely than liberals to believe and thus share fake news or misinformation about issues related to COVID-19 (Calvillo et al. 2020; Lawson and Kakkar 2021). On the other hand, since Republicans and Democrats tend to view each other as distant others, the Third-Person Effect would suggest that they will not perceive they have shared misinformation. (Jang and Kim 2018). This information leads to the following research question:

RQ3: Who is more likely to believe that they have shared false information about the COVID-19 virus, vaccine, or masking, Republicans or Democrats?

Third-Person Effect (Ștefăniță, Corbu and Buturoiu 2018) would suggest that most people will believe that others have shared more misinformation/fake news about issues related to COVID-19, though they will see their friends and family in a better light than distant others, so there may not be a difference between how they perceive themselves and how they perceive their friends and family. This study only examines their views of friends and family, not distant others.

RQ4: Do participants believe that they or their friends and family members have been verbally attacked in the comments when they state their beliefs about the COVID-19 virus, vaccine, or masking?

Some research has suggested that when people are in social media environments where they are exposed to more diverse ideas, they are more likely to check facts (Schuetz, Sykes and Venkatesh 2021). On the other hand, other researchers have found that most people use social media within an echo chamber (Germani and Biller-Andorno 2021; Westerwick, Johnson and Knobloch-Westerwick 2017), where most people share the same beliefs. Given this information, we propose the following research questions:

RQ5a: How well do participants believe they evaluate their sources before sharing information about the COVID-19 virus, vaccine, or masking?

RQ5b: What perceptions do participants have for their own sharing of information or disbelieving of shared information?

The popular press has provided a lot of news about conflict between family members about their responses to the COVID-19 virus, vaccine, and masking policies. For instance, Wolf (Wolf 2021) reported that readers of *The New York Times* have had family relationships torn apart because of disagreements about what the best (most ethical) way is to behave during the global pandemic. Since many family members are seeing each other's beliefs play out on social media, we asked the following research question:

RQ6: Do participants perceive that their own or their family and friends' postings about COVID-19 have affected the participants' perceptions of their friends and family?

Twitter has been called out specifically in scholarly research as a significant source of misinformation (Germani and Biller-Andorno 2021), as have Facebook (Bruns, Harrington and Hurcombe 2020) and YouTube (Stecula and Pickup 2021). Instead of directly looking at the fake news and misinformation promulgated on social media platforms, we wanted to know which platforms users believed were more likely to be the source of shared misinformation or fake news.

RQ7: What platform do participants believe is the greatest source of misinformation about the COVID-19 virus, vaccine, or masking?

METHODS

Participants

We used a convenience sample of respondents who received access to the survey from posts to social media platforms, requests via email to faculty, and through a posting to an emailed newsletter sponsored by the National Communication Association. The majority of the participants who reported demographics were female (67%, N = 133), 32 percent (N = 64) were male, and 1.5 percent (N = 3) were gender nonconforming or preferred not to say. The vast majority of participants reported their race as white (82.8%, N = 173), with 11 (5.2%) reporting they were African American, 6 (2.9%) as Asian, 5 (2.4%) as other, 8 (3.8%) as Hispanic or Latino, 1 (.05%) as American Indian, Native American or Alaskan Native, and 5 (2.4%) who preferred not to disclose.

The age range of the participants was 18–73, with the majority of participants being in the 18–23-year-old age group (N = 101, 55.4%). This age range is likely the most common because the vast majority of the participants in the study were students (N = 236, 80.1%) and many students had the opportunity to earn extra credit if they participated in the study. In the student group (N = 143), 29 (20.3 percent) reported they were first year students, 4.4 percent (N = 14.7) reported they were sophomores, 16.1 percent (N = 23) were juniors, 35.7 percent were seniors (N = 51), 10.5 percent (N = 15) were M.A. students, and 2.8 percent (N = 4) were PhD students. Of the nonstudent population (N = 55), 5.5 percent (N = 3) reported some college credits, but no degree, 34.4 percent (N = 19) reported a bachelor's degree, 24.4 percent (N = 15) noted a master's degree, and 29.1 percent (16) reported they had doctoral degree.

Half (50.1%, N = 220) of participants reported that they had used social media for ten or more years, with 36.2 percent (N = 159) reporting they had used it for six to nine years. Only 13.7 percent (N = 60) reported using it for five or fewer years.

Measures

For the current study, we updated a survey first created by Swenson-Lepper (2011) to examine student perceptions of ethical issues in the use of Facebook and updated in 2019 (Swenson-Lepper and Kerby 2019) to examine communication ethics in a wider variety of social media platforms. Consistent with the previous two surveys, the survey asked for participants to identify how long they have used social media in general, the social media platforms they use and how often they use them, along with basic demographic information. The updated survey asked open-ended questions about the biggest ethical issue they notice related to COVID-19, the vaccine for COVID-19, and masks on social media, along with what they perceived to be the most unethical ways that they've seen social media used in relationship to COVID-19 issues. The survey also asked Likert-type questions about whether they had accidentally shared or believed misinformation about COVID-19, masking, or vaccinations. For instance, one item is "I have believed something about COVID-19 on social media that I believed to be true, but later learned was false" (rated strongly disagree to strongly agree). Further questions asked whether they have felt attacked for sharing opinions about COVID-19, mask wearing, or vaccinations, along with asking them how much they check their sources. Finally, the survey asked participants to identify their political affiliation in order to examine whether there was a relationship between the types of ethical issues they noticed and their political perspective. The complete survey is in the appendix.

Procedure

The Winona State University Institutional Review Board (IRB) approved the Qualtrics survey and research method, and we shared the survey using IRB-approved messages on COMMNotes (the daily message system of the National Communication Association), via email with colleagues at Winona State University and at other universities, and on a wide variety of social media platforms, including Facebook, Instagram, and LinkedIn. After clicking on the link, participants saw a description of the study and they were asked to agree to participate, with their agreement to participate serving as their consent. The median time it took for participants to complete the survey was 19.35 minutes, which means it was a lengthy survey. At the end of the survey participants were asked if they were university students. If they were students in participating classes, they could click on a link at the end to go to a separate survey to identify themselves, their course, and their professor in order to receive extra credit. Nonstudent participants were thanked for their participation and the survey ended.

RESULTS AND DISCUSSION

RQ1a: What do participants believe to be the greatest ethical issue related to the COVID-19 virus, vaccine, or masking on social media?

The primary ethical issues that participants mentioned were misinformation, freedom of speech and other rights, lack of tolerance, politicizing COVID-19, and the rights of the individual versus the needs of the community. Participants were concerned about the spread of misinformation on social media platforms. They talked about this in a variety of ways, but the following are representative quotes:

- *I think the spreading of misinformation is a huge social media issue and it leads to more conflicts between people.*

- *I think the biggest ethical issue is spreading things related to covid (sic) that they have not confirmed true or untrue. It is an issue because too many people use social media as their main source of information.*
- *The biggest misconceptions I have seen pertaining to the vaccine and its relation to the government. I have seen a lot of conspiracies about the government putting harmful chemicals into the vaccine, people saying the vaccine doesn't work at all, or that it causes infertility when there is no evidence to support those claims. I have also seen the controversy between vaccinating young kids and not. I think these are ethical dilemmas as it causes a lot of arguments on social media and in the public. Especially when fear is introduced, people are influenced heavily by their fears.*

People often reference rights or freedom of speech when talking about the COVID-19 vaccine and masking. Some refer to the First Amendment right of freedom of religion, or freedom of speech.

- *Infringing on rights that are covered by the bill of rights (sic). I think there are some things like masks that can and should be enforced. Vaccines on the other hand may blatantly violate religious rights which is protected by the first amendment (all capitalization and punctuation are as they were in the original response).*

People view tolerance or the lack thereof in different ways when thinking about COVID-19, the vaccines, and masking.

- *The biggest ethical issue I have noticed regarding COVID on social media is the intolerance of other opinions and beliefs. Certain narratives have been pushed that those who get the vaccine are ignorant, scared, or brainwashed. Certain narratives have been pushed that those who do not get the vaccine are ignorant, selfish, or entitled.*
- *Many people [assume] their view is the correct and ethical one, allowing for no possibility that others may have good points, too, or that they may be wrong about some of the data they believe they have interpreted correctly.*

The politicizing of COVID-19 and other pandemic-related issues was the key ethical issue discussed by many participants.

- *That Covid-19 in the United States was ever political. It is public health information for a global pandemic—we the people should only be getting information from health experts in the related fields and our government should support our scientists.*

- *The biggest ethical issue is the interest of politics that go along with this virus. There's very obviously two sides that take two different stances on this topic, but it's terrible that these two opinions have very different consequences concerning the virus.*

Some participants noted that there was tension between those who want to protect the community and those who are focused on individual freedoms.

- *I think the biggest ethical issue is the value of health for oneself and others. To many, wearing a mask symbolizes the value of personal health and community health. To others, not wearing a mask symbolizes Americanness and exercising the freedoms of the government. Either way, social media magnifies these two stances because one instance or confrontation with mask-wearing policies can spread like wildfire to those who were never there.*
- *I think it's the question of individual versus community and which should we help? One, both, or neither?*

Another statement, which does not fit the categories of most of the themes, is particularly relevant when talking about communication ethics:

- *The biggest ethical issue is the misunderstood belief that there is nothing more important than an individual's self-defined concept of Personal Freedom (sic), to the extent that there are no consequences for doing ANYTHING wrong, and that my personal freedoms are more important than the health and well-being of any other person.*

RQ1b: What do participants believe are the most unethical ways that they have seen social media used related to the COVID-19 virus, vaccine, or masking?

While many of the responses to this question are similar to the responses found for Research Question 1a, there are some differences worth noting. The key difference is that participants named former president Donald Trump as someone who acted unethically on social media related to the COVID-19 pandemic and focused on the role organized religion played in sharing misinformation. See below for representative quotes.

- *Trump tweets for sure. Any politician using their audience and platform to misinform.*
- *Trump and others like him who have outright denied what scientists and other experts say and who push for others to call names and incited violence on people who disagree with them.*

- *Spreading misinformation is the most obvious answer. But I would also say using it to shame or fame people for wearing masks and getting vaccinated. Trump telling people to drink bleach to get rid of symptoms or expressing that covid isn't that bad is a good example.*
- *Political trumpers (sic) who spread inaccurate vaccine information and risk, while they themselves are getting vaccinated.*

Another area of difference are responses that point out different religious organizations' culpability as sources of misinformation. One person noted:

- *The weaponization of organized religion against vaccination status. Recently, my aunt read posts from an anti-vax Facebook page to me that proclaimed that those who did not "get the jab" were "following God's will" and were part of the "pure blood" race. The posts continued with anti-vaccination rhetoric, based on Christianity, which is incredibly unethical.*
- *To me the most unethical way that social media has been used to misinform people about COVID-19, is the way the religious sectors place fear in their parishioners out of the hope that religion will sway then (sic) to believe the pandemic is a hoax, was created by democrats (sic) or in the ways that religious leaders have swayed people to not get vaccinated.*

RQ2a: Do participants believe that they have believed false information about the COVID-19 virus, vaccine, or masking?

More respondents believe that they have shared information they initially thought was true about COVID-19 (43.4% either strongly or somewhat agreed) but later learned was false than believed that they had done so for either the vaccines for COVID-19 (33.9% either strongly agreed or somewhat agreed) or masking (33.1% either strongly agreed or agreed). In general, participants tend to strongly or somewhat disagree that they have believed misinformation related to the coronavirus (44.3%), the vaccines to prevent COVID-19 (53.1%), and masking (52.4%).

RQ2b: Do participants believe that they or or their friends and family have shared false information about the COVID-19 virus, vaccine, or masking?

Less than 5 percent of respondents strongly or somewhat agreed with statements that they have unintentionally shared fake news or misinformation about the COVID-19 virus, the COVID-19 vaccines, or masking. On the other hand, 61.7 percent (N = 176) strongly or somewhat agreed that their family or friends have shared fake news or misinformation about the COVID-19 virus and COVID-19 vaccines on social media, and 57.5 percent (N = 168) strongly or somewhat agreed that their friends and family have shared misinformation about masking as a preventative strategy against COVID-19.

H1: Based on the Third-Person Effect, participants will believe that their friends and family members have shared more false information about the COVID-19 virus, vaccine, or masking than they have.

The results for a one-tailed t-test were significant ($t=(290)$ -21.03, $p<.001$), indicating that respondents believed that their friends and family members were more likely to share false information than they were.

Research questions 2a and 2b and Hypothesis 1 focused on whether participants believe they or their friends and family have shared false information about the COVID-19 virus, the COVID-19 vaccines, or masking. As the Third-Person Effect (Corbu et al. 2020, Ştefăniță, Corbu and Buturoiu 2018) would suggest, most people believe that they are less likely to have shared fake news or misinformation than their friends or family members. But, as demonstrated by the descriptive statistics in RQ2a, many people are willing to admit that they may have accidentally shared information they later learned was false. Additionally, when participants responded to the item about the most unethical ways that they have seen social media used, many of them cited "Donald Trump" or his followers. This is consistent with what Evanega et al. (2020) note from their quantitative study of misinformation, where they write "the President of the United States was likely the largest driver of the COVID-19 misinformation 'infodemic'" (4).

RQ3: Who is more likely to believe that they have shared false information about the COVID-19 virus, vaccine, or masking, Republicans or Democrats?

There was no significant difference between Republicans and Democrats in their self-reporting of sharing fake news about COVID ($t(165) = -.67$, $p = .503$). Consistent with the Third-Person Effect, the results of RQ3 found Republicans and Democrats showed no difference in their self-reported sharing of fake news or misinformation. Recent research has shown, however, that the most conservative posters are the most likely to share misinformation (Hopp, Ferrucci, and Vargo 2020).

RQ4: Do participants believe that they and their friends and family members have been verbally attacked in the comments when they state their beliefs about the COVID-19 virus, vaccine, or masking?

About a quarter of participants (26.7%) either strongly agree (N = 30) or agree (N = 47) that they have been attacked for posting their beliefs about COVID-19 on social media, but approximately two-thirds (N = 185, 64.0%) either strongly agree or agree that they have witnessed verbal attacks on their friends or families for posting their views about COVID-19. The same holds true for their perceptions of whether they have been attacked (N = 74, 25.7%) for opinions about mask wearing versus whether their friends and family have been attacked (N = 176, 60.9%) and whether they have been attacked for stating their opinions about COVID-19 vaccinations (N = 73, 25.3%) versus whether their friends and family have been verbally attacked (N = 94, 59.7%). Additionally, the majority of participants (N = 185, 64.2%) agree that they have refrained from sharing information related to COVID-19, masking, or vaccines on social media because they feared a negative response from others on social media.

Third-Person Effect would suggest that most people will believe that others have shared more misinformation/fake news about issues related to COVID-19, though they will see their friends and family in a better light than distant others, so there may not be a difference between how they perceive themselves and how they perceive their friends and family. This study only examines their views of friends and family, not distant others.

RQ5a: How well do participants believe they evaluate their sources before sharing information about the COVID-19 virus, vaccine, or masking?

In response to the statement, "If a social media post related to COVID-19 provides sources, I research the sources to ensure their validity," 65.4 percent of respondents either strongly agree (N = 84, 29.4%) or somewhat agree (N = 103, 36.0%) general, participants believe that they research the sources cited on social media. Additionally, the majority (83.9%) of respondents either strongly (N = 156, 54.5%) or somewhat agreed (N = 84, 29.4%) with the statement "I question shared information on social media regarding COVID-19 rather than immediately taking it as face value."

RQ5b: What perceptions do participants have of their own sharing of information or disbelieving of shared information?

Most respondents denied posting information about COVID-19 on social media because their peers or family members posted that information (N = 178, 62%) either strongly or somewhat disagreed), and 81 percent (N = 233) strongly or somewhat disagreed with the statement that they had shared information they didn't agree with because many of their peers or family members had posted the same information. Most (N = 165, 57%) also strongly or somewhat disagreed with this statement: "When information on social media related to COVID-19 does not align with my previous views about COVID-19, I assume it is unimportant or incorrect." Nearly 20 percent (18.8%) somewhat or strongly agreed that they would reshare information that was aesthetically pleasing, though 41 percent strongly disagreed with this statement.

RQ6: Do participants perceive that their own or their family and friends' postings about COVID-19 have affected their perceptions of their friends and family?

About 30 percent of participants (N = 85) either strongly or somewhat agreed that their social media posts about COVID-19 have caused conflict with their family members or friends, while 62 percent (N = 179) either agreed or strongly agreed that postings by friends or family members have caused negative feelings for them. Respondents were much less likely to believe their own posts had caused conflict, compared to the posts of their family and friends ($t = (287) -12.02, p < .001$). While this may have happened because respondents are comparing themselves (one person) to their network (many people with many opportunities to post offensive posts), another explanation for this difference is Third-Person Effect.

Consistent with the Third-Person Effect, the results for research questions five and six showed that almost half of participants believe that their friends and family members have been attacked for posting information about COVID-related issues, but only 30 percent believe that this is true for themselves. This result may occur because participants have opinionated family and friends, or because their networks on social media give them more opportunities to see examples of this behavior. The most interesting finding to come from RQ5b is that almost 20 percent of participants believed that they would reshare information based on its appearance. This is in contrast with the 85 percent who believe that they question shared information.

While we were unable to find scholarly sources about the effects of social media postings about COVID-related issues on family relationships, the popular press (Wolf 2021) has provided examples of this, and this was also supported by our results, where more than a third believed that their own social media posts have caused conflicts with family and friends, and approximately two-thirds of participants believe they have negative feelings toward family and friends because of their postings. This finding shows the relational toll that the pandemic has taken on relationships.

RQ7: What platform do participants believe is the greatest source of misinformation about the COVID-19 virus, vaccine, or masking?

Overall, respondents view Facebook as the social media platform most likely to be a source of misinformation about issues related to COVID-19. Over two-thirds of participants ranked it the number one source of misinformation, while 20 percent ranked it as the second greatest source of information (see table 3.1). Surprisingly, and in contrast to Stecula and Pickup (2021), participants rated YouTube as the second lowest source of misinformation, with Snapchat ranked the lowest source of misinformation by almost all respondents. However, these results are similar to those found by Newman et al. (2021), where they found that in the U.S. Facebook was the greatest platform of concern for misinformation, followed by Twitter, and then YouTube. Their survey did not ask participants about TikTok, Instagram, or Snapchat, but did include WhatsApp, which is not used as widely used in the United States as it is in the rest of the world.

Table 3.1 Social Platforms Ranked by Participants as Sources of Misinformation

Platform	N	Rated Greatest Source of Misinformation (%)	N	Rated Second Greatest Source of Misinformation (%)
Facebook	174	66.9	51	19.6
Twitter	29	11.2	68	26.2
TikTok	26	10.0	43	16.5
Instagram	19	7.3	52	20.0
YouTube	10	3.8	29	11.2
Snapchat	2	0.8	17	6.5

CONCLUSION

Strengths and Weaknesses

The study has significant challenges in terms of its sample; a better sample would be randomly selected from the entire U.S. population and represent all demographic groups. Additionally, our sample consists primarily of college students, who tend to live and work with people like them, amplifying the echo chamber of social media (Germani and Biller-Andorno 2021, Westerwick, Johnson, and Knobloch-Westerwick 2017). Additionally, the survey was probably too long, with the average person completing the survey taking roughly twenty minutes; a considerable number of people started the survey but stopped prior to answering the open-ended questions near the beginning of the survey. Being able to compensate participants would have made it more likely that people would have completed all components of the survey. Another weakness is that we conducted this survey almost two years into the pandemic, during the Omicron wave, when people were cynical about whether the pandemic would end and about the effectiveness of vaccines and masking.

On the other hand, one of the major strengths of this study is that it asks people directly what they believe are the most important ethical issues related to social media and the COVID-19 virus, the vaccines, and masking. As in our previous work (Swenson-Lepper 2011, Swenson-Lepper and Kerby 2019), we believe it is important that the voices of average Americans be heard. Additionally, the open-ended questions provided in-depth insight into the perspectives people have about ethical issues related to the pandemic. Responses show that there is a deep division between people; they believe their rights are threatened or that others are unethical because they are not putting the community first. They also believe misinformation is widespread and that high-quality information is hard to come by. Respondents seem to believe that if enough voices are heard, the truth will rise to the top. They also believe that certain voices have been unethical during the pandemic, including Donald Trump and religious leaders, among others.

Directions for Future Research

One of the interesting findings from this research is the role aesthetics plays in some people's willingness to repost information on social media. Since the aesthetics of social media postings are valued by users, it may work in harmony with their ethical values or serve as a tension for ethical decision-making. Additionally, had we known the pandemic would stretch on so long, it would have been interesting to see how Americans' views of ethics and misinformation changed over time in relation to the COVID-19 virus, vaccines, and masking. More work also could have been done to examine political ideology and ethical perspectives in this context.

In sum, we examined U.S. residents' perceptions of misinformation and ethics in social media related to the COVID-19 pandemic, which has not been studied in the current literature. In an online survey, participants (N = 290) noted their perceptions on the ethics of posting about COVID-19, masking, and the COVID-19 vaccines. They were also asked open-ended questions about their perspectives on misinformation and fake news as they relate to COVID-19, masking, and vaccines. Consistent with the main ideas of the Third-Person Effect, most people believe their friends and family are more likely to share misinformation than they are. Participants believed that the most important ethical issues about social media and the pandemic were misinformation, freedom of speech and other civil rights, lack of tolerance, politicizing COVID-19, and the rights of the individual versus the needs of the community. People hold widely varying views of their own and others' rights, which leads to ethical tensions that should be studied further.

REFERENCES

Abraham, Betina, and Megha Mandalaparthy. 2021. "Fake News during Covid-19 Outbreak: Differentiating Audience's Age regarding Prior, Exposure, Emotion, Susceptibility, Practice, and Forwarding Behaviour." *Media Watch* 12, no. 2: 251–64. doi: 10.15655/mw/2021/v12i2/160150.

Alba, Davey. 2021. *Facebook Groups Promoting Ivermectin as a Covid-19 Treatment Continue to Flourish.* September 28. www.nytimes.com/2021/09/28/technology/facebook-ivermectin-coronavirus-misinformation.html.

Apukea, Oberiri Destiny, and Bahiyah Omara. 2021. "Fake News and COVID-19: Modelling the Predictors of Fake News Sharing among Social Media Users." *Telematics and Informatics* 56: e101475. doi: 10.1016/j.tele.2020.101475.

Ardèvol-Abreu, Alberto, Patricia Delponti, and Carmen Rodríguez-Wangüemert. 2020. "Intentional or Inadvertent Fake News Sharing? Fact-Checking Warnings and Users' Interaction with Social Media Content." *Profesional de la Información* 29, no. 5: e290507. doi: 10.3145/epi.2020.sep.07.

Atehortua, Nelson A., and Stella Patino. 2021. "COVID-19, a Tale of Two Pandemics: Novel Coronavirus and Fake News Messaging." *Health Promotion International* 36: 524–34. doi: 10.1093/heapro/daaa140.

Auxier, Brooke, and Monica Anderson. 2021. "Social Media Use in 2021." *Pew Research Center.* April 7. www.pewresearch.org/internet/2021/04/07/social-media-use-in-2021.

Baek, Young Min, Hyunhee Kang, and Sonho Kim. 2019. "Fake News Should Be Regulated Because It Influences Both "Others" and "Me": How and Why the Influence of Presumed Influence Model Should Be Extended." *Mass Communication & Society* 22, no. 3: 301–23. doi: 10.1080/15205436.2018.1562076.

Bagdasarov, Zhanna, April Martin, Rahul Chauhan, and Shane Connelly. 2017. "Aristotle, Kant, and . . . Facebook? A Look at the Implications of Social Media on Ethics." *Ethics & Behavior* 27, no. 7: 547–61. doi: 10.1080/10508422.2016.1269648.

Banning, Stephen A. 2006. "Third-Person Effects on Political Participation." *Journalism and Mass Communication Quarterly* 83, no. 4: 785–800. doi: 10.1177/107769900608300404.

Berriman, Liam, and Rachel Thomson. 2015. "Spectacles of Intimacy? Mapping the Moral Landscape of Teenage Social Media." *Journal of Youth Studies* 18, no. 5: 583–97. doi: 10.1080/13676261.2014.992323.

Bond, Shannon. 2020. *'The Perfect Storm': How Vaccine Misinformation Spread to the Mainstream.* NPR, December 10. www.npr.org/2020/12/10/944408988/the-perfect-storm-how-coronavirus-spread-vaccine-misinformation-to-the-mainstream.

———. 2021. *Just 12 People Are behind Most Vaccine Hoaxes on Social Media, Research Shows*. NPR, May 14. www.npr.org/2021/05/13/996570855/disinformation-dozen-test-facebooks-twitters-ability-to-curb-vaccine-hoaxes.

Bratu, Sofia. 2020. "The Fake News Sociology of COVID-19 Pandemic Fear: Dangerously Inaccurate Beliefs, Emotional Contagion, and Conspiracy Ideation." *Linguistic and Philosophical Investigations* 19: 128–34. doi: 10.22381/LPI19202010.

Bruns, Axel, Stephen Harrington, and Edward Hurcombe. 2020. "'Corona? 5G? or Both?': The Dynamics of COVID-19/5G Conspiracy Theories on Facebook." *Media International Australia* 177, no. 1: 12–29. doi: 10.1177/1329878X20946113.

Bumsoo, Kim. 2020. "Effects of Social Grooming on Incivility in COVID-19." *Cyberpsychology, Behavior, and Social Networking* 23, no. 8: 519–25. doi: 10.1089/cyber.2020.0201.

Calvillo, Dustin P., Bryan J. Ross, Ryan J. B. Garcia, Thomas J. Smelter, and Abraham M. Rutchick. 2020. "Political Ideology Predicts Perceptions of the Threat of COVID-19 (and Susceptibility to Fake News about It)." *Social Psychological and Personality Science* 11, no. 8: 1119–28. doi: 10.1177/1948550620940539.

Cartwright, Luke. 2017. "Supporting Students to Use Social Media and Comply with Professional Standards." *Social Work Education* 36, no. 8: 880–92. doi: 10.1080/02615479.2017.1372409.

Casero-Ripollés, Andreu. 2020. "Impact of Covid-19 on the Media System. Communicative and Democratic Consequences of News Consumption during the Outbreak." *El profesional de la información* 29, no. 2: e290223. doi: 10.3145/epi.2020.mar.23.

Corbu, Nicoleta, Denisa-Adriana Oprea, Elena Negrea-Busuioc, and Loredana Radu. 2020. ""They Can't Fool Me, but They Can Fool the Others!" Third Person Effect and Fake News Detection." *European Journal of Communication* 35, no. 2: 165–80. doi: 10.1177/0267323120903686.

Davison, W. Phillips. 1983. "The Third-Person Effect in Communication." *Public Opinion Quarterly* 47: 1–15.

de Beaumont Foundation. 2021. "Study: Americans Who Get COVID-19 Information from Social Media More Likely to Believe Misinformation, Less Likely to Be Vaccinated." *debeaumont.org*. November 4. https://debeaumont.org/news/2021/social-media-misinformation-poll.

Demiray, A., M. Cakar, A. Acil, N. Ilaslan, and T. Savas Yucel. 2020. "Social Media Use and Ethics Violations: Nurses' Responses to Hypothetical Cases." *International Nursing Review* 67, no. 1: 84–91. doi: 10.1111/inr.12563.

Drouin, Michelle, Kimberly W. O'Connor, Gordon B. Schmidt, and Daniel A. Miller. 2015. "Facebook Fired: Legal Perspectives and Young Adults' Opinions on the Use of Social Media in Hiring and Firing Decisions." *Computers in Human Behavior* 46: 123–28. doi: 0.1016/j.chb.2015.01.011.

Du, Erhu, Eddie Chen, Ji Liu, and Chunmiao Zheng. 2021. "How Do Social Media and Individual Behaviors Affect Epidemic Transmission and Control?" *Science of the Total Environment* 761: 144114. doi: 10.1016/j.scitotenv.2020.144114.

Evanega, Sarah, Mark Lynas, Jordan Adams, and Karinne Smolenyak. 2020. "Coronavirus Misinformation: Quantifying Sources and Themes in the COVID-19

'Infodemic.'" Cornell Alliance for Science. https://allianceforscience.cornell.edu/wp-content/uploads/2020/09/Evanega-et-al-Coronavirus-misinformationFINAL.pdf.

Germani, Federico, and Nikola Biller-Andorno. 2021. "The Anti-Vaccination Infodemic on Social Media: A Behavioral Analysis." *PLOS One* 16, no. 3: e0247642. doi: 10.1371/journal.pone.0247642.

Gerosa, Tiziano, Marco Gui, Eszter Hargittai, and Minh Hao Nguyen. 2021. "(Mis) informed During COVID-19: How Education Level and Information Sources Contribute to Knowledge Gaps." *International Journal of Communication* 15: 2196–2217.

Grace, Pamela J. 2021. "Nurses Spreading Misinformation." *AJN American Journal of Nursing* 121 (12): 49–53. doi: 0.1097/01.NAJ.0000803200.65113.fd.

Greene, Ciara M., and Gillian Murphy. 2020. "Individual Differences in Susceptibility to False Memories for Covid 19 Fake News." *Cognitive Research* 5, no. 63: 1–8. doi: 10.1186/s41235-020-00262-1.

Hokke, Stacey, Naomi J. Hackworth, Shannon K. Bennetts, Jan M. Nicholson, Patrick Keyzer, Jayne Lucke, Lawrie Zion, and Sharinne B. Crawford. 2020. "Ethical Considerations in Using Social Media to Engage Research Participants: Perspectives of Australian Researchers and Ethics Committee Members." *Journal of Empirical Research on Human Research Ethics* 15 (1/2): 12–27. doi: 10.1177/1556264619854629.

Hopp, Toby, Patrick Ferrucci, and Chris J. Vargo. 2020. "Why Do People Share Ideologically Extreme, False, and Misleading Content on Social Media? A Self-Report and Trace Data–Based Analysis of Countermedia Content Dissemination on Facebook and Twitter." *Human Communication Research* 46: 357–84. doi: 10.1093/hcr/hqz022.

Hunter, Ruth F., Aisling Gough, Niamh O'Kane, McKeown, Aine McKeown, Tom Walker, Michelle McKinley, Mandy Lee, and Frank Kee. 2018. "Ethical Issues in Social Media Research for Public Health." *American Journal of Public Health* 108, no. 3: 343–48. doi: 10.2105/AJPH.2017.304249.

Hwang, Yongsuk, and Osung Kwon. 2017. "A Study on the Conceptualization and Regulation Measures on Fake News—Focused on Self-Regulation of Internet Service Providers." *Journal of Media Law, Ethics and Policy Research* 16, no. 1: 53–101. doi: 10.26542/JML.2017.4.16.1.53.

Jang, S. Mo, and Joon K. Kim. 2018. "Third Person Effects of Fake News: Fake News Regulation and Media Literacy Interventions." *Computers in Human Behavior* 80: 295–302. doi: 10.1016/j.chb.2017.11.034.

Lawson, M. Asher, and Hemant Kakkar. 2021. "Of Pandemics, Politics, and Personality: The Role of Conscientiousness and Political Ideology in the Sharing of Fake News." *Journal of Experimental Psychology: General* Advance Online Publication. 1–24. doi: 10.1037/xge0001120.

Lee, Francis L. F. 2010. "The Prevention Effect of Third-Person Perception: A Study on the Perceived and Actual Influence of Polls." *Mass Communication and Society* 13, no. 1: 87–110. doi: 10.1080/15205430802635672.

Lee, Hyunmin, and Sun-A Park. 2016. "Third-Person Effect and Pandemic Flu: The Role of Severity, Self-Efficacy Method Mentions, and Message Source." *Journal of Health Communication* 21: 1244–50. doi: 10.1080/10810730.2016.1245801.

Liu, Piper Liping, and Lei Vincent Huang. 2020. "Digital Disinformation about COVID-19 and the Third-Person Effect: Examining the Channel Differences and Negative Emotional Outcomes." *Cyberpsychology, Behavior, and Social Networking* 23, no. 11: 789–93. doi: 10.1089/cyber.2020.0363.

Matsa, Katerina Eva, and Sarah Naseer. 2021. "News Platform Fact Sheet." *Pew Research Center*. November 8. www.pewresearch.org/journalism/fact-sheet/news-platform-fact-sheet.

Michaelidou, Nina, and Milena Micevski. 2019. "Consumers' Ethical Perceptions of Social Media Analytics Practices: Risks, Benefits and Potential Outcomes." *Journal of Business Research* 104: 576–96. doi: 10.1016/j.jbusres.2018.12.008.

Mulvey, Gerald J., K. Deleon, and Brad Sowder. 2020. "Social Media Ethics for the Meteorologist." *Bulletin of the American Meteorological Society* 101, no. 8: 723–25. doi: 10.1175/BAMS-D-19-0226.1.

Newman, Nic, Richard Fletcher, Anne Schulz, Simge Andl, Craig T. Robertson, and Rasmus K. Nielsen. 2021. "Reuters Institute Digital News Report, 10th ed." Reuters Institute for the Study of Journalism. https://reutersinstitute.politics.ox.ac.uk/digital-news-report/2021/dnr-executive-summary.

O'Connor, Kimberly W., Gordon B. Schmidt, and Michelle Drouin. 2016. "Suspended Because of Social Media? Students' Knowledge and Opinions of University Social Media Policies and Practices." *Computers in Human Behavior* 65: 619–26. doi: 10.1016/j.chb.2016.06.001.

Ognyanova, Katkherine, David Lazer, Matthew A. Baum, James Druckman, Jon Green, Roy H. Perlis, Mauricio Santillana, Jennifer Lin, Matthew Simonson, and Ata Usla. 2021. "The COVID States Project: A 50 State COVID-19 Survey: Report #60: Vaccine Misinformation, from Uncertainty to Resistance." August. https://news.northeastern.edu/uploads/COVID19%20CONSORTIUM%20REPORT%2060%20MISINFO%20August%202021.pdf.

Pennycook, Gordon, Jonathon McPhetres, Yunhao Zhang, Jackson G. Lu, and David G. Rand. 2020. "Fighting COVID-19 Misinformation on Social Media: Experimental Evidence for a Scalable Accuracy-Nudge Intervention." *Psychological Science* 31, no. 7: 770–80. doi: 10.1177/0956797620939054.

Perloff, Richard M. 1999. "The Third-Person Effect: A Critical Review and Synthesis." *Media Psychology* 1: 353–78.

Preston, Stephanie, Anthony Anderson, David J. Robertson, Mark P. Shephard, and Narisong Huhe. 2021. "Detecting Fake News on Facebook: The Role of Emotional Intelligence." *PLOS ONE* 16, no. 3: e0246757. doi: 10.1371/journal.pone.0246757.

Quinn, Emma K., Sajjad S. Fazel, and Cheryl E. Peters. 2021. "The Instagram Infodemic: Cobranding of Conspiracy Theories, Coronavirus Disease 2019 and Authority-Questioning Beliefs." *Cyberpsychology, Behavior, and Social Networking* 24, no. 8: 573–77. doi: 10.1089/cyber.2020.0663.

Ramjug, Peter. 2021. *How False Information Could Be Affecting COVID-19 Vaccination Rates.* August 10. https://news.northeastern.edu/2021/08/10/how-false-information-could-be-lowering-covid-19-vaccination-rates.

Rattani, Abbas, and Amelia Johns. 2017. "Collaborative Partnerships and Gatekeepers in Online Research Recruitment." *American Journal of Bioethics* 17, no. 3: 27–29. doi: 10.1080/15265161.2016.1274800.

Roozenbeek, Jon, Alexandra L. J. Freeman, and Sander van der Linden. 2021. "How Accurate Are Accuracy-Nudge Interventions? A Preregistered Direct Replication of Pennycook et al. (2020)." *Psychological Science* 32, no. 7: 1169–78. doi: 10.1177/09567976211024535.

Salwen, Michael B., and Michel Dupagne. 2001. "Third-Person Perception of Television Violence: The Role of Self-Perceived Knowledge." *Media Psychology* 3, no. 3: 211–36. doi: 10.1207/S1532785XMEP0303_01.

Schuetz, Sebastian W., Tracy Ann Sykes, and Viswanath Venkatesh. 2021. "Combating COVID-19 Fake News on Social Media through Fact Checking: Antecedents and Consequences." *European Journal of Information Systems* 30, no. 4: 376–88. doi: 10.1080/0960085X.2021.1895682.

Schweisberger, Valarie, Jennifer Billinson, and T. Makana Chock. 2014. "Face, the Third-Person Effect, and the Differential Impact Hypothesis." *Journal of Computer-Mediated Communication* 19: 403–13. doi: 10.1111/jcc4.12061.

Stavrositu, Carmen D., and Jinhee Kim. 2014. "Social Media Metrics: Third-Person Perceptions of Health Information." *Computers in Human Behavior* 35: 61–67. doi: 10.1016/j.chb.2014.02.025.

Stecula, Dominik A., and Mark Pickup. 2021. "Social Media, Cognitive Reflection, and Conspiracy Beliefs." *Frontiers in Political Science* 3: 647957. doi: 10.3389/fpos.2021.647957.

Ștefăniță, Oana, Nicoleta Corbu, and Raluca Buturoiu. 2018. "Fake News and the Third-Person Effect: They Are More Influenced Than Me and You." *Journal of Media Research* 3, no. 32: 5–23. doi: 10.24193/jmr.32.1.

Swenson-Lepper, Tammy. 2011. "Facebook: Student Perceptions of Ethical Issues about Their Online Presence." In *The Ethics of Emerging Media: Information, Social Norms, and New Media Technology*, edited by Bruce E. Drushel and Kathleen German, 175–88. New York: Continuum.

Swenson-Lepper, Tammy, and April Kerby. 2019. "Cyberbullies, Trolls, and Stalkers: Students' Perceptions of Ethical Issues in Social Media." *Journal of Media Ethics* 34, no. 2: 102–13. doi: 10.1080/23736992.2019.1599721.

Tayal, Pulkit, and Vijayakumar Bharathi S. 2021. "Reliability and Trust Perception of Users on Social Media Posts Related to the Ongoing COVID-19 Pandemic." *Journal of Human Behavior in the Social Environment* 31, no. 1–4: 325–39. doi: 10.1080/10911359.2020.1825254.

Tiffany, Kaitlyn. 2020. "Something in the Air." *The Atlantic.* www.theatlantic.com/technology/archive/2020/05/great-5g-conspiracy/611317.

Tsay-Vogel, Mina. 2016. "Me versus Them: Third-Person Effects among Facebook Users." *New Media & Society* 18, no. 9: 1956–72. doi: 10.1177/1461444815573476.

Van der Meer, Toni G. L. A., Michael Hameleers, and Anne C. Kroon. 2020. "Crafting Our Own Biased Media Diets: The Effects of Confirmation, Source, and Negativity Bias on Selective Attendance to Online News." *Mass Communication and Society* 23, no. 6: 937–67. doi: 10.1080/15205436.2020.1782432.

Vitriol, Joseph A., and Jessecae K. Marsh. 2021. "A Pandemic of Misbelief: How Beliefs Promote or Undermine COVID-19 Mitigation." *Frontiers in Political Science* 16, no. 3: e648082. doi: 10.3389/fpos.2021.648082.

Wei, Ran, Ven-Hwei Lo, Hung-Yi Lu, and Hsin-Ya Hou. 2015. "Examining Multiple Behavioral Effects of Third-Person Perception: Evidence from the News about Fukushima Nuclear Crisis in Taiwan." *Chinese Journal of Communication* 8, no. 1: 95–111. doi: 10.1080/17544750.2014.972422.

Westerwick, Axel, Benjamin K. Johnson, and Silvia Knobloch-Westerwick. 2017. "Confirmation Biases in Selective Exposure to Political Online Information: Source Bias vs. Content Bias." *Communication Monographs* 84, no. 3: 343–64. doi: 10.1080/03637751.2016.1272761.

Wolf, Jonathan. 2021. "Coronavirus Briefing: Covid Family Feuds." *New York Times*, December 28. www.nytimes.com/2021/12/28/briefing/covid-briefing.html.

Wood, Daniel. 2021. "Pro-Trump Counties Now Have Far Higher COVID Death Rates. Misinformation Is to Blame." NPR, December 5. www.npr.org/sections/health-shots/2021/12/05/1059828993/data-vaccine-misinformation-trump-counties-covid-death-rate.

Wright, Chrysalis L., and Hang Duong. 2021. "COVID-19 Fake News and Attitudes toward Asian Americans." *Journal of Media Research*, 14, no. 1: 5–29. doi: 10.24193/jmr.39.1.

Wu, Katherine S., and Janet L. Sonne. 2021. "Therapist Boundary Crossings in the Digital Age: Psychologists' Practice Frequencies and Perceptions of Ethicality." *Professional Psychology: Research and Practice* 52, no. 5: 419–28. doi: 10.1037/pro0000406.

Xie, Guang-Xin. 2016. "Deceptive Advertising and Third-Person Perception: The Interplay of Generalized and Specific Suspicion." *Journal of Marketing Communications* 22, no. 5: 494–512. doi: 10.1080/13527266.2014.918051.

Yang, Fan, and Michel Horning. 2020. "Reluctant to Share: How Third Person Perceptions of Fake News Discourage News Readers from Sharing 'Real News' on Social Media." *Social Media + Society* 6, no. 3: 1–11. doi: 10.1177/2056305120955173.

Yang, Jeongwon, and Yu Tian. 2021. "'Others Are More Vulnerable to Fake News Than I Am': Third-Person Effect of COVID-19 Fake News on Social Media Users." *Computers in Human Behavior* 125: 106950. doi: 10.1016/j.chb.2021.106950.

Part II

SOCIAL MEDIA, COVID-19, AND WELL-BEING

Chapter 4

Exploring the Impact of COVID-19 on Leisure through Social Media

Annette M. Holba

Social media are here to stay; there is no denying this claim. If it will be our partner in our lives, we need to understand how social media impact the human experience and the human condition. One way to understand how social media impact the human experience is to consider its role in leisure practices in our daily lives. With leisure being a necessary part of the human experience, looking at social media's role in leisure experiences can be helpful. What is even more helpful is to consider the experience of social media during a time of deep and widespread crisis in the human experience. The purpose of this chapter is to explore what we have learned about how people engaged social media as leisure during the global COVID-19 pandemic.

Coming from a classical understanding of leisure that posits the first principle of all action is leisure (Aristotle 2001b), I begin by briefly discussing the idea that leisure is the basis of culture, and that leisure is significant to the human condition. Then, I explore the emerging literature on how the circumstances of the COVID-19 global pandemic were impacted by social media. Next, I focus on the role and use of social media related to leisure and the specific social conditions during the pandemic. Finally, I attempt to identify outcomes and future considerations pertaining to leisure and social media from what we now have learned about the impacts of a global pandemic on leisure experiences and spaces. This chapter will demonstrate the value of leisure to our well-being as individuals and as participants in human cultures, affirming Josef Pieper's (1998) claim that leisure is the basis of culture.

During late fall of 2019, people were already getting sick with an unidentified virus. In December 2019, that unidentified and unnumbered novel coronavirus was already taking hold through observations of a variety of formidable outbreaks in various locations across China, most notably in Wuhan, China, but then spreading across Thailand, the Republic of Korea,

Japan, the United States, the Philippines, Vietnam, and Taiwan. By February 2020, this new virus was found in twenty-five countries (Wu, Chen, and Chan 2020). At this time, the news coverage began to cover these observations, and people were dying. On February 11, 2020, the WHO identified this new virus as COVID-19; prior to this, the Taiwan CDC had already named the virus Severe Pneumonia with Novel Pathogens (Wu, Chen, and Chan 2020). According to Scott LaFee (2021), it is likely that COVID-19 was already substantially circulating for two months before the first human case in Wuhan emerged in December 2019. This means it is likely the virus was already spreading undetected across China. On March 11, 2020, the WHO declared COVID-19 as a worldwide pandemic (Havitz, Pritchard, and Dimanche 2021). By April 2020, COVID-19 was found in more than 100 countries worldwide and death tolls were rising (LaFee 2021). At this time, many colleges and universities in the United States were either on spring break or anticipating spring break. Consequently, it was around March and April of 2020 that the decision was made to shut down all educational institutions—primary, secondary, and colleges and universities. This was the beginning of significant disruptions that would impact the global economy and people's individual daily lives around the world (Jamison and Wang 2021). What we saw were rolling economic and social lockdowns. People all over the country and the world stayed home; offices were closed, schools were closed, and restaurants were closed. The only organizations that remained open were those in the essential service industries such as police, fire, hospitals, and grocery stores to name just a few. To remain open, these organizations were required to implement significant protocols to ensure workers would be safe at work. This was just the beginning. Fast forward to June 2022, according to the CDC COVID Data Tracker, in the United States alone, we identified 84,565,697 COVID-19 cases and to date, 1,003,803 have died, that we know of, from COVID-19.

COVID-19 is a very serious virus. Fortunately, the medical professionals, clinicians, researchers, and scholars worked together and quickly developed three main vaccines that ultimately were distributed across the country and around the world. As the United States worked tirelessly to get people vaccinated, the virus mutated over and over again, the mask mandates came and went, and we are now experiencing what some researchers refer to as a shift from pandemic to endemic, which means the virus is now part of our environment, like the flu is part of our environment. We do not know for certain about the future, but we might anticipate living with COVID-19 as we live with the annual flu. During the last two years, people in the United States and all around the world were told to stay inside, stay home, and socialization was discouraged. So, what did people do? We know many people either worked from home or stopped working. Additionally, the United States government sent three stimulus checks that were designed to help people eat/survive during and after the economic shutdowns. We know that there were moratoriums on evictions and other supportive policies or restrictions that were implemented so that people would not lose their homes or starve. Healthcare even changed as the increase in telehealth services helped people to maintain their health. We are slowly coming to terms with learning to live with less severe versions of COVID-19. It is now time to see what we can learn about how we really handled this pandemic in our social and intimate lives. How did COVID-19 impact people's experiences with leisure in the first two years of the pandemic? Furthermore, did social media play a role in how leisure was experienced during the COVID-19 pandemic, and if so, what was that role? Before examining these two questions, I first lay out the importance of leisure experiences and spaces to the human condition.

LEISURE AS THE BASIS OF CULTURE AND THE HUMAN CONDITION

While I might disagree with some definitions of leisure or the conflation of leisure and recreation, I do believe that no matter how one defines or understands leisure, during the COVID-19 global pandemic, most people came to realize leisure took on a new significance in managing, negotiating, and understanding the human experience during the global crisis of a pandemic (Lashua, Johnson, and Parry 2021). Today, our impressions about leisure are often drawn toward thoughts of happiness, the good life, resting or relaxation of the mind and body, and, to some extent, the freedom to do nothing. In some cultures, leisure is often thought of as engaging in recreative or non-work activities, or refraining from doing anything at all. But whatever we think about leisure, we must remain open to leisure as affording possibilities of transformation. Josef Pieper (1998) explains how leisure is considered the basis and the foundation of culture; he states that leisure has had a negative rap from the puritans and the protestant work ethic that Max Weber (1905) advocates, which dictates one ought to always be producing something and that idle hands are just excuses for the devil to take hold (Holba 2013). Pieper (1998) states that leisure cultivates the soul of those who engage it because the practice of leisure requires contemplative action; Pieper indicates these people will be more likely to cultivate *Bildung*, the German word for culture that is enriched by academic education. Leisure creates the conditions for the existence of culture. Leisure trains the mind for the health of one's intellectual life. Leisure promotes deep thinking which enables one to contribute to the larger society in healthy ways. Leisure creates the condition for culture to emerge and it cultivates the human interiority so that humans can be effective with others, meeting others where they are in constructive and positive ways. Leisure enables people to think, reflect, and organize their lives to live together in an interdependent experience with others. The ability to contemplate ideas at deeper levels is a byproduct of practicing leisure. Leisure enables one to cultivate habits of patience, humility, and reflective engagement. These are qualities that get lost in our fast-paced, immediacy-focused public realm (Honore 2005). Leisure prepares our minds to think deeply and see the larger picture before coming to judgment. This is how leisure contributes to the development of culture.

Hannah Arendt (1958), social and political philosopher from the twentieth century, suggested that leisure is important because it provides the opportunity to engage in reflective thought which enlarges one's thinking. This is a necessary component of one's public life. Arendt (1958) discussed the human condition in relation to work, action, and labor. Leisure, for Arendt, would be associated with labor, the things we do to sustain life. In other words, leisure is a necessity to feed and sustain life processes. This is true for both the individual and the entire human species. This is a very different form of work for Arendt. Work, in this case, refers to what Arendt referred to as "unnaturalness" which is working for a living, that daily toil we do to earn a living and pay the rent (Arendt 1958, 7). Working for a living is unnatural because it builds things that can actually outlast the human life processes. Leisure as labor is life giving and life sustaining. Leisure cultivates the inner self, one's interiority, and in doing so this prepares one to engage with other humans. The only way we sustain human existence is to live together in a community. Leisure, in the sense of labor, cultivates our interiority and intellect. It fosters hermeneutic humility, the ability to be present, and meditative or reflective thinking, all in alignment with life processes and human existence. Without the labor of leisure, Arendt's understanding of action cannot be fulfilled because action requires other human beings. Action is how we work together with others that maintain the public domain and create the society in which we live together.

Beyond these philosophical underpinnings around leisure, contemporary, pragmatic, and critical views of leisure suggest that "leisure impacts us as [a] public cultural construct rife with ideals, tastes, and beliefs that we may not share nor want" (Mowatt 2021, 44). With this said, scholars suggest that leisure during the COVID-19 pandemic is a "complicated and problematic reality" that both hides and reveals the toxic implication of competing ideals, tastes, and values (Mowatt 2021, 44). Some suggest that during COVID-19, leisure became the enemy (Mowatt 2021). One reason for this perspective is the broad-based lockdown and stay-at-home orders. Rasul Mowatt (2021) suggests that the mere experience of being forced to stay at home increased the potential for domestic violence and abuse. Additionally, Mowatt (2021) claims that being in public can be just as threatening as staying at home with an abuser since the lack of resources, increasing frustration with the pandemic, and other public orders such as masking increase the potential for person-to-person harms in public settings. Other social media researchers identify the addictive nature of social media platforms especially on traditional college-age individuals (Avenduk 2021). Even with some of these negative effects of social media engagement, not everything about social media is negative.

Today, it is widely acknowledged that leisure is an important activity that affects everyone's life, especially since it is attributed to increasing the quality of life and an individual's general overall happiness (Avunduk 2021). Leisure is often identified with freedom to choose what one wants to do, and it offers opportunities for relaxation, diversion, and self-reflection (Sivan 2020). It is clear that leisure activities are sharply separated from one's working-for-a-living activities.

Leisure affords sustained attention to an activity, to-the-thing-itself, and this experience is not hampered by time, telos, or a predetermined or anticipated outcome. What I mean by time as it relates to leisure is that time is experienced as a *time outside of time* (Guignon and Aho 2010). This is similar to the Greek concept of Kairos. Kairos can be described as a timeliness or an opportune time. Leisure is also guided by a hermeneutical mindset—a mindset that acknowledges openness and engaging in an activity for the sake of itself. Leisure is a transformative experience that allows one to transcend the mundane and the obvious and it is a way of life, not just a moment in time that interrupts work (Holba 2007, 2013). Leisure as a way of life mirrors what Pierre Hadot (1995) refers to as spiritual exercises—these are approaches to experiences that cultivate one's inner self. Leisure is absolutely necessary for the cultivation of the inner self. This is not a new conversation. Plato and Aristotle also wrote about the significance of cultivating the inner self because it is tied to enlarged thinking and having a philosophical mindset. In "The Republic," Plato (1984) states that when one thinks, one is talking with their soul. This reflects a deep and significant process that cannot be superficial. Talking with one's soul means that one is deeply looking within the self as the soul is conceptually deep within the human being's inner landscape. This is the backdrop of Plato's philosopher king, one who thinks deeply and also has political acumen and acuity. Aristotle (2001a) elevated contemplation to the highest form of human activity because when we contemplate, we engage in a deep and unique act of human reasoning. Thinking deeply is necessary for finding truth and experiencing happiness. Hannah Arendt (1958) also espoused the need for an active contemplative life that would cultivate enlarged thinking. For Arendt (1958), enlarged thinking is not just for engaging in the public realm, especially politics, but it is also central to how human beings engage with each other. Enlarged thinking is a necessary ethic between self and other.

Sustained attention to leisure enlarges one's aesthetic sensibilities that can ward off negative communication habits. Leisure provides an inner defense against being enslaved by the culture of narcissism and the communicative behavior of emotivism (Holba 2014, 2022). A richer understanding of narcissism goes beyond self-love. Christopher Lasch (1979) describes narcissism in terms of individuals being stuck in self-absorption, unable to move forward or sometimes backward in their relationships, or at work, or in other areas of their lives. Lasch (1979) describes this as being in "purely personal preoccupations," unable to recognize and tend to the needs of others around them (4). These individuals who are stuck are unable to help themselves even though they might focus on self-help practices that actually keep them tied to their present state of being. They do not notice their stuckness and this creates a false sense of self that is unsatisfying. This means they remain in their self-absorption mindset and are unable to find a real way out of it. Leisure provides distance from this self-absorption and is one way that can dislodge one from their own narcissism. Leisure can do the same for the individual who is stuck within an emotivistic mindset.

Alasdair MacIntyre (2007) indicates that narcissism creates such a sense of loss and abandonment that it brings the individual to be driven by emotivism. Emotivism in this sense projects a narcissism that discounts the autonomy of the other—it is an ethical violation of the other that attempts to manipulate the other to thinking, doing, and being like one's own self (MacIntyre 2007). Emotivism totally disregards the autonomy of the other and demands the other to be like oneself. Emotivism is truly dangerous because it rejects the authenticity and existence of the other. Leisure expands one's horizons, moving away from creating any negative impact upon the other and the risk of getting stuck in narcissism and emotivism. Leisure provides hermeneutic openings that recognize and celebrate ideas, learning, and thinking with others. This prepares one's ground for ethical engagement with the other. Having this understanding of leisure is helpful to the overall sentiment of this chapter. The next section lays out, in general terms, social media and its usage during the pandemic.

COVID-19, LOCKDOWNS, AND SOCIAL MEDIA

Framing how this chapter defines social media and describing social media usage, in general, informs the next section about how to consider the role of social media in leisure practices during the pandemic. Social media have been defined by Kaplan and Haelen (2010) as an internet-based application that builds on the technological and ideological foundation of Web 2.0. It also allows for the creation of user-generated content which makes it possible for participatory public engagement (Kaplan and Haenlen 2010). As online environments, social media enable people to "introduce themselves in a social environment, and share their ideas, thoughts, photos, and videos with other people" (Avunduk 2021, 508). In the most recent years, due to advancements in technologies, smartphones, computers, and tablets have become indispensable in our daily lives for people to work, play, and live their lives (Avunduk 2021). It is also well-supported that using social media is the most preferred kind of activity during one's leisure time (Sheth 2020). During the COVID-19 global pandemic, social media took on an increasingly more important role that most people would have never imagined due to widespread, and at some points, global public space lockdowns. This means that for many people, the only way to remain connected to other human beings was through the internet and specifically, using social media platforms where they could see others visually, either through pictures (Facebook or LinkedIn) or virtually (Facebook Messenger Video Chat) or other virtual meeting or video conferencing platforms. Especially during the waves of COVID-19 lockdowns and the limits or constraints implemented across most industries, people had to find different ways to stay connected to others.

Social media became a crucial communication tool during the lockdowns that have come to define the COVID-19 global pandemic (Tsao et al. 2021). Social media platforms contributed to this crucial role of global communication. Platforms such as Facebook, Instagram, TikTok, Snapchat, and Pinterest were used to keep people connected, updated, and informed. People created their own YouTube channels to keep in touch with family, communicate information, and express political perspectives during high stake events such as the murder of George Floyd by a Minneapolis police officer and large events around the Black Lives Matter (BLM) initiatives. While initially during the COVID-19 disruption, funerals were delayed for those people who died from COVID or other causes, eventually, once funeral services started back up, people could share funeral information with others through social media sites (MacNeil et. al 2021). Music was also shared through YouTube and other sites for school and youth musical productions (Fram et al. 2021). Many schools live streamed productions with no in-person audiences and many music teachers held concerts over video conferencing platforms, such as Stageit.com, or continued with music lessons in these virtual spaces (Billboard Staff 2021).

Even today as I write this chapter, while the COVID-19 infection numbers and rates have lowered and slowed in the United States, China is again dealing with excessively high numbers and lockdowns across Shanghai and Beijing. The infection rates are so high that people have been locked down for the last two months from wherever they are, whether they are at work or at home. As of June 1, 2022, Shanghai finally released the forced lockdown and people are again able to move about the city with a little more freedom but still using a mask.

To clarify what it means to shut down or have lockdowns, Panarese and Azzarita (2021) define them as closure of all nonessential workplaces, suspension of all face-to-face teaching in schools (primary, secondary, and college levels), and various other restrictions on all kinds of physical or in-person social interactions, from playgrounds to libraries to amusement parks and beaches. The CDC website listed the following infrastructure workers as essential, thus requiring people working in these fields to continue working as safely as possible during the lockdowns, healthcare and public health workers, transportation system employees and those who maintain these systems, information technology, nuclear reactors and waste systems, water systems, government facilities, financial systems, emergency services, defense systems, food and agriculture, critical manufacturing, chemical plants, energy systems and some communication systems.

Due to these widespread public space closures, many people, especially younger generations, had to identify adaptation strategies in order to try to maintain their lifestyle choices, at least as much as they could within the various restrictions most communities experienced. These adaptations would come to have impacts not only on their lifestyles but also their well-being (Panarese and Azzarita 2021). It was partially through digital technologies that people compensated for the restrictions and limitations that the lockdowns caused on social relations. As an example, with the closing of many public spaces, people had to become creative. Many middle and high schools canceled their graduation ceremonies but not all of them. Many graduations were conducted virtually with only the graduates walking across the stage to get their diplomas in front of an empty field or auditorium. These were sometimes live streamed for families and friends to watch. Some schools held drive by graduations where students stayed in their vehicles as they were driven in a caravan line. Many of these creative modes of graduation were captured and shared over a variety of social media sites to acknowledge loved ones publicly and to include family members who would have been present otherwise (Sparks 2020). Many churches did similar things, livestreaming a Mass or Service and sharing the videos across social media. For some churches, they may continue providing this service; for others, it was a substitute until people could once again come together in social relations (Pillay 2020). The term social distancing became prevalent in the media from the experts at the World Health Organization (WHO) and the Centers for Disease Control (CDC), and across the digital landscape. While some experts tried to correct the couplet to more accurately denote the requested action to physical distancing, the fact is the couplet social distancing went viral and the correction never fully held (Allen, Ling, and Burton 2020).

It was the action of social distancing that might have had the most profound and disproportionate effect on the younger age groups who were in their early development phases and still developing, because they relied on social interaction as a vital means of their overall development into adulthood. There would need to be some kind of replacement activity to support development because the body could not organically stop developing. While the lockdown drastically altered people's ability to have social and physical interactions, their social and physical habits also changed (Panarese and Azzarita 2021). One of the most significant areas of experiences that have significant effect on youth and young adult development is the leisure experience that often occurs through social interaction with one's peers. This general understanding of social media opens the discussion to explore the role of social media around leisure during the COVID-19 global pandemic.

LEISURE, SOCIAL MEDIA, AND COVID-19: WHAT WE LEARNED

Social media have become almost fully integrated into most people's everyday lives, regardless of the domain of engagement, such as work, home, or play. This means that social media's role has begun to be redefined through a broader cultural experience—it is not just a communication tool. While the uses of social media have many different aims, contexts, and practices, some scholars suggest that some social media practices can be considered leisure and playful which is the opposite of specific social networking practices that focus more on functionality and tasks (Albrechtslund and Albrechtslund 2014). This reframing of social media was already starting to occur before March 2020, when the announcement came that we were in a global pandemic and the lockdowns began. Instead of just being a useful tool that can maintain social networks and connections, social media was on the verge of becoming a useful, and useless, thing or activity which provided opportunities for basic human meaning-making—which is what leisure can bring forth.

One example of the value of totally useless things comes from Roland Barthes's (2013) discussion of the Eiffel Tower, something the builder envisioned as useful, though it has never been used for anything but a tourist attraction (Albrechtslund and Albrechtslund 2014). Even though it does nothing functional or task-oriented, it does hold the space for imagination, social gatherings, aesthetic attunement, and other tangible and intangible experiences. We can see how the totally useless, deemed this way from a utilitarian perspective, can at once become a haven for useful, open, and serendipitous experiences. While the Eiffel Tower is a physical phenomenon, Albrechtslund and Albrechtslund (2014) identify the nonphysical phenomenon in what they refer to as "leisurely online sociality" which is a touristic practice that reinvents how we understand the uses of social media in the context of tourism. Online tourism, or virtual tourism and digital tourism, generally refers to viewers who are potential physical tourists and who have an immersive experience exploring destinations through various technologies. These technologies include the internet, social media, video conferencing, and digital maps, to name just a few. These technologies are used as tools to gather, organize, manage, and prepare for travel or some kind of immersive experience with a particular culture or cultures in the broadest sense. Scholars suggest online tourism also involves experiencing pleasure and joy from the experience of using these tools (Majeed et al. 2020).

Online sociality refers to practices that are similar to ordinary experiences we do in person that involve sharing experiences with others through conversation or other actions and behaviors to make social connections or build relationships. The difference is that they are done online in digital spaces. These practices would include posting text on social media sites, uploading images, creating digital content to share with others, and other sharing of personal information on a public site. This blends the public and the private realm together. While this could cause confusion if the information is not clear, it can also build relationships since the private realms were limited or closed to others (Albrechtslund and Albrechtslund 2014). This leisurely online sociality was instrumental especially during the COVID-19 lockdowns. Some people might initially believe that online tourism is not tourism at all but what it does is prepare one for a possible future physical touristic experience all the while preparing one visually for the experience as well as providing information that aids in the organizing of one's time during the experience. The digital tools available to inform the public about physical places better prepare one for the experience and provide the opportunity to the consumer to engage in the experience to some extent prior to a firsthand experience. For some, this might be considered a useless activity, but in reality, it actually enhances one's experience because it ensures one's preparedness for a later time. We might also reframe the value of what is considered "useless" and change this belief.

There have been long-standing discussions around the need for useless, needless, and purposeless activities (Ramsey 2011; Willems and Aalders 2021). These seemingly useless practices are the practices that actually create meaning and have an aesthetic usefulness for the inner being and for the sake of itself (Schiller 2016). This kind of sentiment is contrary to Max Weber's (1905) Protestant work ethic which focuses on intentionality and productive output of an activity, thus privileging work over play. The idea behind emphasizing the useless, needless, and purposeless is twofold. First, these activities provide distanciation, taking distance from something focused and intense (Schrag 2003). Distance is considered as a place of respite, a recovery of sorts that allows one to be refreshed and ready for reengagement. It helps to step out of intensity and then step back into it rejuvenated. Second, stepping away from something allows one to see the thing stepped away from through a different perspective; it is a kind of reorientation. Distanciation allows for some disinterestedness to inform one's positionality in healthy ways (Gadamer 2004). In both distanciation and disinterestedness, one gains perspective even if it appears to look like one is doing nothing. It requires, in fact, a very busy mindset to do nothing.

Before the COVID-19 pandemic hit the world, we already knew that social media, in general, had a significant impact on leisure awareness, activities, and access (Aydin and Arslan 2016). This is especially significant for the recreation and tourism industries. Studies suggest that social media is instrumental to both passive and active forms of leisure (Aydin and Arslan 2016). Active leisure refers to bodily activity, physical movement, and active engagement in the physical environment; passive leisure refers to activity via social media (Aydin and Arslan 2016). Though, passive leisure, such as flipping through a Facebook feed with a finger and reading postings of others with a bit of interest but having no long-term commitment is very different from playing online games such as the Nintendo Wii or Pokémon Go, two interactive online games that involve significant physical activity. Through social media platforms, one can find varying experiences of leisure that may be passive or active at differing levels. The leisure activities most likely to be engaged during the pandemic would likely be those activities that are doable from home (Morse, Fine, and Friedlander 2021). Some of these activities would include gardening and DIY maintenance and there are different ways of adding a social media component to both of these kinds of experiences, such as using apps to identify certain plants and chat with other people who have had the same plants. DIY apps provide experiences for people of all ages such as DIY: The Social Learning App is for children through teenagers and Redecor—Home is an app for adults who want to learn and practice redesigning their home spaces. Passive leisure usually involves less engagement with interactivity and others than active leisure but both experiences are still leisure experiences.

Leisure activities at home were more likely due to people being at home more for reasons including working from home, having reduced commuting time away from home, and the lockdowns or stay-at-home mandates that kept people in their home environment (Morse, Fine, and Friedlander 2021). While activities across different countries would vary, there was also a difference between people who were active before COVID-19 and those who were less active before COVID-19. For example, a Belgium study found that people who were generally more active before the pandemic actually increased their activity more than those people who were not more active before the pandemic (Morse, Fine, and Friedlander 2021). Additionally, due to COVID-19 restrictions, people spent more time on other leisure activities including home crafts, mind games, learning languages, social food and relaxation, IT interests, fine arts, and performing arts (Morse, Fine, and Friedlander 2021).

Albrechtslund and Albrechtslund (2014) articulate a nuanced understanding of the activities connecting everyday life and social media during COVID-19 restrictions. They suggest it can be encouraging and motivating for people to learn to engage in social media uselessly in order to gain the benefits of having a leisure experience (Albrechtslund and Albrechtslund 2014). They argue that if we engage social media uselessly, this means we should not have purposefulness in our social media engagement. When we have specific outcomes in mind from leisure activities, those expectations tend to create constraints or limits on our activity. While we usually need boundaries and purposefulness in our work life in order to produce what we need to produce at work, in our leisure experiences, these kinds of expectations more often limit the experience from reaching a fuller potential. For example, if I am going to read a book because someone told me in the story something supernatural happens then I will tend to read to look for that particular scene or storyline. By reading with this intention or purpose, I likely will miss other facets of the story that build other parts of the narrative for which my understanding of the story will be incomplete. By having no intentions other than to read the story, while it might feel useless or purposeless, I am able to absorb the narrative more completely. This uselessness is a key feature of leisure as it releases one from the demands so frequently held over us. So often today, engagement on social media has become politically motivated with specific purposefulness which fills the space with overbearing or toxic ideas that can cause anger, anxiety, and stress. It is the intention that shifts one from uselessness to purposefulness, and this is not helpful or healthy to one's mindset, one's physicality, or one's relationships.

It is safe to say that the literature tells us COVID-19 transformed people's leisure behaviors in general (Leon, Rodas, and Greer 2021). This is particularly true for certain specific populations. For example, incarcerated youths in juvenile detention centers experienced similar mental health issues as many non-incarcerated juveniles. However, their opportunities for engaging in leisure were limited compared to non-incarcerated youth. During COVID-19, volunteers who might bring in leisure activities into detention facilities were no longer allowed to enter the facilities or they refused to enter the facilities due to fear of or uncertainty about the virus. This meant that correctional facility staff had to take on those roles even if they were not particularly interested or skilled in different leisure areas. Some detention centers offered leisure activities around virtual music classes, letter or card writing, and some physical activities (Leo, Rodas, and Greer 2021). Although, any activity within the confines of a detention center would also be limited by space constraints and cleaning/maintaining equipment or resources.

One year into the global pandemic, researchers studying human dynamics studied how human beings were handling social connectedness, social networks, and screen time as they relate to an individual's mental health, or as Pandya and Lodha (2021) refer to it, an individual's digital mental health; they point out that through the physical lockdowns, the digital terrain was the only space in which people could stay connected and have reciprocal engagement. The lockdowns restricted most social interactions outside of one's location, whether home or work, which led to the overuse of digital devices for socializing, virtual tourism, virtual parties, and family gatherings (Dé, Pandey and Pal 2020).

Of course, we know that human interaction is essential for the human species to survive and thrive. Social media provided a conduit for human interaction to continue in a digital realm that once felt optional but actually became vital. For example, prior to COVID-19, our grandchildren would come for weekends quite often. This gave their parents some time alone on weekends and it provided my husband and I an opportunity to have fun time with our grandchildren that allowed us to fully focus on them. Pre-COVID-19 we had our grandchildren monthly and occasionally we would FaceTime them during the week. Once the lockdowns started and before we knew much about COVID-19, for at least one year we did not have our grandchildren sleep over or even come physically over to our house. So, while FaceTime was optional pre-COVID-19, once COVID-19 settled in as a danger, it became a vital tool to help us stay connected with our grandchildren. We started to FaceTime with them daily so we could stay connected with them. We also began to play Roblox on our tablets so that we could play games with them. Roblox is a virtual universe that you build and share experiences with other players. We played this game with them almost every day, too. FaceTime and Roblox became vital to our relationships with our grandchildren.

A paradox emerged within this context since outdoor face-to-face leisure activities were restricted and while the same leisure activities moved or adapted to digital environments, it was still the case that youth and younger adults simply had more free time on their hands than ever before. Some researchers consider that this excess of free time is akin to forced leisure and it meant that there was no choice whether or not to engage in leisure; one was simply forced into an unstructured space of leisure (Panarese and Azzarita 2021). This meant that whether you wanted it or not, you could do nothing else, like work, unless you worked in an essential field, which most youth and young adults did not. According to Panarese and Azzarita (2021) unstructured leisure could be considered a waste of time if it does not morph into a structured leisure. But the structured leisure Panarese and Azzarita (2021) refer to is not a restricted structure that would limit one's experience; rather, it is an imaginative and open structure that would allow the activity to unfold unhampered. It is only when one could structure their leisure activity in an unhampered way, even if it was through digital structuring, that one would truly benefit from leisure as Josef Pieper envisioned leisure cultivating one's soul, spirit, or interiority. Structured leisure would have an overarching framework to it, such as activities outside of school time programs, including experiences around sports, arts, and social interactions (Panarese and Azzarita 2021). Additionally, Panarese and Azzarita (2001) claimed though that unstructured leisure did less to contribute to their physical, social, and emotional development, especially in youth. However, some form of structured leisure had life-affirming benefits. For example, if we consider structured leisure as participation on a regular basis, scheduled within one's day, with a focused agenda or goal, and some kind of guided interaction that focuses on building skills and receiving some kind of feedback, we can identify unstructured leisure as an experience ungoverned in this same way. When I think about this distinction, I remember for ten years, as an adult, I took private violin lessons once per month. My hour-long lessons included learning scales and arpeggios, working on the difficult parts of my orchestra music, and building my concerto repertoire by learning one or two violin concertos per year, and being required to give a recital every year. This was my leisure, not my work. I scheduled lessons in my calendar, I knew what I had to learn and work on, I received feedback from my teacher, and I met my goals each year; this was life-affirming for me. These lessons actually made me a better sight reader in orchestra, and I also began playing in a string quartet. When I played in the quartet, we had fairly regular but flexible meeting times but usually we had no idea what we would play from week to week. Unstructured leisure had less constraints and allowed flexibility in a more focused way, though in both activities I learned a lot but very different things. In structured leisure, I learned specific concerto literature and gained valuable recital performance experience, both of which built my confidence musically. My unstructured leisure experiences helped me to be a better general musician but nothing more specific.

Generally, the potential for leisure to benefit individuals during a global pandemic holds great promise, though it is not without unique and pressing challenges (Mowatt 2021). Many of the studies conducted around how people spent their time during the first year to eighteen months of the pandemic did not define leisure activities other than to indicate activities people did during lockdowns when they could not leave their homes to go to work or to play.

This means that the researchers did not look for leisure activities that would align with Josef Pieper's very uncompromising definition of leisure as a philosophical act or an intellectual cultivation of the soul. However, what is interesting to note is that most of the studies did share an understanding that leisure activities did increase, and they did so through digital practices and spaces. Keeping this flexible understanding of leisure in mind, we can see that the role of social media was significant to the experience and contours of leisure during the COVID-19 landscape.

While unstructured leisure might create less significant positive impacts on individuals, during COVID-19 when everything was closed or when large gatherings were not permitted, unstructured leisure could be a lifeline to many people just needing and seeking human connection. Leisure in any form provided this lifeline and most of the time it was through social media apps that leisure experiences were engaged. So, instead of critiquing the uselessness of social media, it became the pathway vital to human persistence under very stressful conditions.

Some of the themes around leisure experiences during the lockdowns were described as virtual tourism, leisure screen time, video gaming, video chatting, watching movies, browsing social network sites, and exercising (such as yoga) (Aymerich-Franch 2020). While individuals could stay connected with others through their digital devices and different forms of social media, the downside to being connected primarily through digital space had some negative consequences such as irritability, corona-anxiety, sleep problems, emotional exhaustion, isolation, social media fatigue and screen fatigue, and phantom vibration syndrome (Gurvich et al. 2021; Lodha and DeSousa 2020; Hudimova 2021).

Studies show that during the first year of the COVID-19 pandemic, there was an increase in traditional media and social media consumption (Panarese and Azzarita 2021). The only mediated activity that did not see a dramatic increase was watching conventional TV and listening to the radio, though watching or listening to news did increase. The most significant social media engagement increases included video calling family and friends. A study conducted by Panarese and Azzarita (2021) revealed 81.5 percent of people under twenty-five years of age in Spain maintained connection with family and friends through their cellular phones or through social media apps such as WhatsApp, a cross-platform messaging application that allows people using different device brands to message across any device.

Their study also showed 74.9 percent of people under twenty-five years of age streamed movies and other digital content for leisure and 72.2 percent engaged with social media and messaging services as their leisure. Another study conducted by Laura Aymeric-Franch (2020) indicated that 62.5 percent participants reported watching Netflix or similar streaming platforms, while

60.1 percent reported engaging in social media text-based groups. Interestingly, 59 percent of participants reported activities on social media other than texting, such as posting, reading, viewing images or videos, and following live activities (Aymeric-Franch 2020).

Studies also found that online activities were high for younger people, wherein they tried to do what they considered normal activities but adapted them for online engagement (Panarese and Azzarita 2021). This might involve activities such as learning something new, socializing, meeting new people, or doing one's favorite activity such as yoga. While people were finding new ways to do more traditional activities and stay connected to others, the use of social media technologies only partly mitigated the negative effects of the lockdowns (Panarese and Azzarita 2021). We now know that mental health problems increased during the pandemic (Haddad et al. 2021). We also know that social media could not replace physical interpersonal connections that might help to address many of the mental health problems people faced, but it became clear that social media could play a role in keeping people connected, which to some degree, was able to positively impact at least some of the mental health problems that emerged (Haddad et al. 2021). Some of the most popular social media sites during the pandemic included Facebook, YouTube, WhatsApp, Facebook Messenger, Instagram, WeChat, TikTok, Kakao, Douyin, Sina Weibo, Telegram, Snapchat, Reddit, Pinterest, Twitter, and Quora (Haddad et al. 2021). Social media as a tool to foster connections during periods of isolation, occurred during the beginning of the pandemic, and had positive implications but using social media to access news about the pandemic caused more negative side effects such as increased anxiety and depression (Haddad et al. 2021). So, we can see social media played a serious role during the pandemic but depending upon how one used social media, the experience could garner both negative and positive effects.

Certain activities were reported as being engaged more often than other activities during the initial lockdowns. These activities include reading for leisure and doing activities with other people in their home (Aymerich-Franch 2020). Other activities include doing nothing, getting physical exercise, cleaning the house, using social media, having group social media video-calling chats, streaming TV, cooking or baking, playing board games, spending time with their children and with their pets, and sitting outside for fresh air and sun (Aymerich-Franch 2020). Some researchers suggest that the usage of social media was increased due to the need for overcoming isolation and seeking alternative methods of connecting with others. Also, during the lockdowns, having nothing else to do, having more free time pushed people to do more on social media platforms (Aymerich-Franch 2020). Overall, it was found that there was a large increase in new digital social media consumption as well as legacy media, those more traditional channels of media such as print and traditional television (Aymerich-Franch 2020). The largest increase in digital consumption was social media engagement and video calling. The social media messaging application most used was WhatsApp (Aymerich-Franch 2020).

It is clear that the pandemic has changed social media, perceptions, usage, and our understanding of it. Some people stopped using Facebook, some people used Peloton and its digital services to get in shape; people flocked to new social platforms such as TikTok and it became clear during the pandemic that our daily interactions were more often mediated by screens (Molla 2021). We also saw that social media usage served as a "social lifeline" as well as a conduit for receiving a wealth of information notifying the world about the trajectory and all issues related to the pandemic (Molla 2021, 2). The pandemic also contributed to the health and sustainability of social media platforms that were starting to wane in interest, such as Facebook, and in many ways, because of social media, people started coming back together after several years of social fragmentation around the world (Molla 2021).

In the United States, Americans spent an average of eighty-two minutes per day using social media apps, which is a seven-minute increase from 2019 (Molla 2021). This study does not break down those users into passive or active social media users. We cannot tell if people posted more as it does vary between platforms and people; however, many people reported scrolling more but posting less. The scrolling action instead of posting may have been a safer way to engage social media because during the pandemic as we saw a rise in cancel culture as well, most of which occurred through social media platforms as they became more politically active, such as Twitter. Those people who did observe they were posting more on social media saw it as an outlet for releasing pent-up boredom, loneliness, or needing to release creativity. For many, social media gave them a psychological comfort, such as not being alone in the pandemic or providing a sense of being able to do something to help with the pandemic which when initially the pandemic broke out, there was an overwhelming sense of not knowing what to do. For example, especially for people who live alone, social media enabled having virtual dinner with others, attending a birthday party virtually, and other socially connecting experiences. Knowing that others, whether living alone or with others, felt the same sense of not knowing what to do helped some to feel supported and connected. Some people also changed their opinions about social media from before the pandemic (Molla 2021). For example, prior to the pandemic, social media was considered a necessary evil that had to be controlled and time on it needed to be limited; however, through the pandemic they reconsidered their attitudes toward social media and changed it to "time well spent" (Molla 2021, 4).

According to Rani Molla (2021), in 2020, misinformation flooded social media from all perspectives. Much of this had to do with negative political campaigning but it also permeated most social, nonpolitical environments too. Many people already had perceptions of social media as toxic environments or a place where conspiracy theories were propagated. However, in 2020, user growth on TikTok dramatically increased and 57 percent of people surveyed had positive sentiment toward TikTok while 43 percent of people surveyed maintained a negative sentiment. Prior to the pandemic, there were more people who had a negative sentiment toward TikTok (Molla 2021). The pandemic allowed people more time to experiment with and discover social media platforms that might be less divisive or polarizing because, at the same time, Facebook was more politically polarizing around political and pandemic issues. Molla (2021) also provided these comparisons across social media platforms. TikTok observed a 576 percent increase in average monthly visits in 2020, while Instagram had a 43 percent increase, Twitter experienced a 36 percent increase, and finally, Facebook only saw a 3 percent increase in monthly visits. At the same time, Facebook beat out TikTok with the length of time users spent on social media when it found users spent an average of 34.6 minutes on its platform while TikTok users only spent 32.8 minutes. The average time spent on other platforms was similar. For example, Twitter, 32.7 minutes; Instagram, 29.6 minutes; and Snapchat, 27.7 minutes. Molla (2021) observed there is now an uptick in preference to engage in livestreaming on various platforms so that the real, unedited, real-time posts can be shared and felt immediately and in more authentic ways.

Additionally, during the height of the pandemic in 2020–2021, people found niche social media-based sites that they are now referring to "social+" such as Clubhouse, Nextdoor, and Goodreads (Molla 2021). These are projected to be the next trending choices gaining much traction. Social+ is a philosophy and a practice that refers to organizations that integrate social connections through digital practices into their business. This means that organizations that integrate social connections into their work life will keep employees satisfied and committed to the organization because social platforms are integrally infused into their employees' lives—keeping employees connected to others at work. This makes it easy for companies to grow and not worry so much about attrition. Examples are companies that integrate social+ applications in their work environment. Some of these applications could be Venmo (easy ways to share funds at work with coworkers), exercise applications (so employees can exercise together), and introducing video-game music in the office environment. These things are familiar to many people and create connections across all employees, and studies suggest that companies that integrate social components into the work environment will continue to thrive while other companies that do not acknowledge the social components will begin to fail (Kim 2022). Because of the immense integration of social media in our lives during the pandemic, it is now embedded in our average lives more than ever before. Live streaming and social entertainment on social media sites, such as TikTok, will likely continue to grow and perhaps evolve. Some projections suggest that while time spent on social media might dip somewhat in the coming years, it will still remain at a higher level than before the pandemic took hold in 2019 (Molla 2021). What we have learned from the choices we made during the last two years of the pandemic is that the increased use of social media increased people's valuations of those and other digital services (Jamison and Wang 2021). We also learned that participating in leisure activities can improve stress-related growth and quality of life. Therefore, it is important to maintain a positive attitude toward any kind of leisure participation, in-person, or digital (Han and Sa 2022).

Social media continue to play a significant role in keeping people informed and connected. The use of social media have been identified as affecting and supporting attitudes, infodemics, the ability to assess mental health, predict COVID cases, analyze government responses, and evaluate the quality of health information (Tsao et al. 2021). Additionally, using social media does a lot more than inform or predict. It brings people together as a fairly structured form of leisure which allows people to build and maintain their relationships, provides a potentially new way to engage in leisure activities, and all of this can aid in the mental health crisis we saw an increase during COVID-19 lockdowns. While not all social media usages can advance the message that they are positively helpful to individuals in every given case, there are hopeful outcomes that demonstrate digital forms of leisure can have benefits, especially during an unprecedented global crisis.

CONCLUSION

This chapter explored the role of social media as leisure during the COVID-19 global pandemic. At the writing of this chapter, we are learning to live with COVID-19 as some medical experts suggest we have rounded the corner as the pandemic is now endemic—we can live with it just like we live with the seasonal flu. It may be too early to trust this conclusion, though it does feel that way right now. One thing we learned early on during the pandemic is that you have to be flexible because what you think you know one day changes the next day. As the research into all facets of the pandemic is continuing, with each new publication we are learning more and more about the social and emotional effects of global lockdowns, social/physical distancing, and mask wearing. Understanding how social media usage was impacted by the pandemic is important because it is clear that the social media terrain is only expanding and becoming more and more integrated into the physicality of our daily lives.

There are some interesting and noteworthy points we can garner from looking at social media usage during COVID-19. First, social media usage expanded across age groups by generations but was particularly influential among younger adults. Second, some studies still found damage from social media or at least its failure to help or relieve individuals from experiencing mental health crises during the global health, social, and economic crises during the pandemic. Third, social media allowed for more creativity and adaptation of mundane practices in developing leisure activities. Fourth, the use of social media and research into understanding its impact reopened the discussion around the value of uselessness—that we need some uselessness in our daily lives for our own well-being, mental health, and physical wellness. Fifth, looking into the role of social media also opened the discussion about structured and unstructured leisure and their implications for the human spirit or condition. These are all important factors as we continue to understand leisure and its impact on the human condition.

What struck me the most in exploring the emergent literature is that there is no one definition of leisure that researchers share. Many of the studies do not define leisure other than equating it to time away from work. But we do a lot of different activities when we are not working. Some of these activities include resting, napping, relaxation, and outdoor recreational activities or indoor recreational activities such as watercolor painting. So, it is really difficult to find consensus around what is meant by the term leisure. While this conundrum is not solvable, nor should it be, it is clear that leisure is life sustaining and community sustaining.

Going back to Josef Pieper's understanding of leisure as the basis of culture, it is really the leisure one does that defines the culture. Moving into the twenty-first century, we clearly see there is a place for leisure in a digital form—if nothing else, this is what the pandemic has taught us. We should make room in our lives for leisure in the digital landscape because leisure is not really about the thing that one does, rather, it is about the nature of the experience. Whether digital (virtual) or analog (physical), leisure is really defined by the mindset we bring to the experience. How one approaches the experience matters, and for leisure one's phenomenological focus of attention must be on the-thing-itself—we can ask ourselves, are we present with the thing that we are doing? Do we see what is before us and are we able to contemplate deeply and reflect on our experiences with it? These are the important aspects of leisure. If we tend to social media through a focused mindset with a contemplative mind, social media usage can only open the possibilities for leisure in the lives of all people who access this emergent digital spatiality.

REFERENCES

Allen, Harris, Brent Ling, and Wayne Burton. 2020. "Stop Using the Term 'Social Distancing'—Start Talking about 'Physical Distancing, Social Connection.'" *Health Affairs Forefront Blog*, April 27. www.healthaffairs.org/do/10.1377/forefront.20200424.213070/full.

Arendt, Hannah. 1958. *The Human Condition*. Chicago: University of Chicago Press.

Aristotle. 2001a. "Nicomachean Ethics." In *The Basic Works of Aristotle*, edited by Richard McKeon, 935–1126. New York: Modern Library.

———. 2001b. "Politics." In *The Basic Works of Aristotle*, edited by Richard McKeon, 1127–1324. New York: Modern Library.

Avunduk, Yesim. 2021. "The Relationship between Leisure Satisfaction and Social Media Addictions of Individuals at University." *Journal of Educational Issues* 7, no. 1: 507–22. doi: 10.5296/jei.v7i1.18592.

Aydin, Bulent, and Erdal Arslan. 2016. "The Role of Social Media on Leisure Preferences: A Research on the Participants of Outdoor Recreation Activities." *Tourism Academic Journal* 3, no. 1: 1–10.

Aymerich-Franch, Laura. 2020. "COVID-19 Lockdown: Impact on Psychological Well-Being and Relationship to Habit and Routine Modifications." *PsyArXiv Preprints*. https://psyarxiv.com/9vm7r.

Barthes, Roland. 2013. *Mythologies*. Translated by Richard Howard and Annette Lavers. New York: Hill and Wang.

Billboard Staff. 2021. "Here Are All the Livestreams & Virtual Concerts to Watch during Coronavirus Crisis." Billboard. www.billboard.com/music/pop/coronavirus-quarantine-music-events-online-streams-9335531.

Centers for Disease Control. n.d. "COVID Data Tracker." Accessed April 29, 2022. https://covid.cdc.gov/covid-data-tracker/#datatracker-home.

Dé, Rahul, Neena Pandey, and Abhipsa Pal. 2020. "Impact of Digital Surge during Covid-19 Pandemic: A Viewpoint on Research and Practice." *International. Journal of Information Management* 55: 1–5. https//doi.org/10.1016/j.ijinfomgt.2020.102171.

Fram, Noah R., Visda Goudarzi, Hiroko Terasawa, and Jonathan Berger. 2021. "Collaborating in Isolation: Assessing the Effects of the COVID-19 Pandemic on Patterns of Collaborative Behavior among Working Musicians." *Frontiers in Psychology* 12: 674246. doi: 10.3389/fpsyg.2021.674246.

Gadamer, Han-Georg. 2004. *Truth and Method*. New York: Continuum.

Guignon, Charles, and Kevin Aho. 2010. "Phenomenological Reflections on Work and Leisure in America." In *The Value of Time and Leisure in a World of Work*, edited by Mitchell R. Haney and A. David Kline, 25–38. Baltimore, MD: Lexington.

Gurvich, Caroline, Natalie Thomas, Elizabeth Hx Thomas, Abdul-Rahman Hudaib, Lomash Sood, Kali Fabiatos, Keith Sutton, Anton Isaacs, Shalini Arunogiri, Gemma Sharp, and Jayashri Kularni. 2021. "Coping Styles and Mental Health in Response to Societal Changes during the COVID-19 Pandemic." *International Journal of Social Psychiatry* 67, no. 5: 540–49. doi: 10.1177/0020764020961790.

Haddad, J. M., Christina Macenski, Alison Mosier-Mills, Alice Hibara, Katherine Kester, Marguerite Schneider, Rachel Conrad, and Cindy H. Lu. 2021. "The Impact of Social Media on College Mental Health During the COVID-19 Pandemic: A Multinational Review of the Existing Literature." *Current Psychiatry Reports* 23: 70. doi: 10.1007/s11920-021-01288.

Hadot, Pierre. 1995. *Philosophy as a Way of Life*. New York: Wiley-Blackwell.

Han, Jee Hoon, and Hye Ji Sa. 2022. "Leisure Attitude, Stress-Related Growth, and Quality of Life during COVID-19-Related Social Distancing." *Social Behavior and Personality: An International Journal* 50, no. 2. doi: 10.2224/sbp.11015.

Havitz, Mark, Mark P. Pritchard, and Frédéric Dimanche. 2021. "Leisure Matters: Cross Continent Conversations in a Time of Crisis." *Leisure Sciences* 43, no. 1–2: 323–29.

Holba, Annette M. 2007. *Philosophical Leisure: Recuperative Praxis for Human Communication*. Milwaukee, WI: Marquette University Press.

———. 2013. *Transformative Leisure: A Philosophy of Communication*. Milwaukee, WI: Marquette University Press.

———. 2014. "In Defense of Leisure." *Communication Quarterly* 62, no. 2: 171–92.

———. 2022. *Philosophy of Communication Inquiry: An Introduction*. San Diego, CA: Cognella.

Honore, C. 2005. *In Praise of Slowness: Challenging the Cult of Speed*. New York: HarperOne.

Hudimova, A. 2021. "Adolescents' Involvement in Social Media: Before and During COVID-19 Pandemic." *International Journal of Innovative Technologies in Social Science* 1, no. 29: 1–11. doi: 10.31435/rsglobal_ijitss/30032021/7370.

Jamison, Mark A., and Peter Wang. 2021. "Valuation of Digital Goods during the Coronavirus Outbreak in the United States." *Telecommunications Policy* 45: 102126. doi: 10.1016/j.telpol.2021.102126.

Kaplan, Andreas M., and Michael Haenlein. 2010. "Users of the World, Unite! The Challenges and Opportunities of Social Media." *Business Horizons* 53: 59–68.

Kim, John S. 2022. "We're Building a Social+ World, but How Will We Moderate It?" *TechCrunch+*. https://techcrunch.com/2022/02/04/were-building-a-social-world-but-how-will-we-moderate-it.

LaFee, Scott. 2021. "Novel Coronavirus Circulated Undetected Months before First COVID-19 Cases in Wuhan, China." Press Release, March 18. https://health.ucsd.edu/news/releases/Pages/2021-03-18-novel-coronavirus-circulated-undetected-months-before-first-covid-19-cases-in-wuhan-china.aspx.

Lasch, C. 1979. *The Culture of Narcissism: American Life in an Age of Diminishing Expectations*. New York: Norton.

Lashua, Brett, Corey W. Johnson, and Diana C. Parry. 2021. "Leisure in the Time of Coronavirus: A Rapid Response Special Issue." *Leisure Sciences* 43, no. 1–2: 6–11.

Leon, Maria, Kevin Rodas, and Mora Greer. 2021. "Leisure behind Bars: The Realities of COVID-19 for Youth Connected to the Justice System." *Leisure Sciences* 43, no. 1–2: 218–24.

Lodha, Pragya, and Avinash De Sousa. 2020. "Mental Health Perspectives of COVID-19 and the Emerging Role of Digital Mental Health and Telepsychiatry." *Archives of Medicine and Health Sciences* 8, no. 1: 133. doi: 10.4103/amhs.amhs_82_20.

MacIntyre, A. 2007. *After Virtue: A Study in Moral Theory.* Notre Dame, IN: Notre Dame University Press.

Mac Neil, A., Blythe Findlay, Rennie Bimman, Taylor Hocking, Tali Barclay, and Jacqueline Ho. 2021. "Exploring the Use of Virtual Funerals During the COVID-19 Pandemic: A Scoping Review." *Omega: Journal of Death and Dying*: 1–24. doi: 10.1177/00302228211045288.

Majeed, Salman, Zhinmin Zhou, Changboa Lu, and Haywantee Ramkissoon. 2020. "Online Tourism Information and Tourist Behavior: A Structural Equation Modeling Analysis Based on a Self-Administered Survey." *Frontiers in Psychology* 11: 1–15. doi: 10.3389/fpsyg.2020.00599.

Molla, Rani. 2021. "Posting Less, Posting More, and Tired of It All: How the Pandemic Has Changed Social Media." *Vox.* www.vox.com/recode/22295131/social-media-use-pandemic-covid-19-instagram-tiktok

Morse, K. F., Phillip A. Fine, and Kathryn J. Friedlander. 2021. "Creativity and Leisure during COVID-19: Examining the Relationship Between Leisure Activities, Motivations, and Psychological Well-Being." *Frontiers in Psychology* 12: 1–22. doi: 10.3389/fpsyg.2021.609967.

Mowatt, Rasul A. 2021. "A People's Future of Leisure Studies: Leisure with the Enemy Under COVID-19." *Leisure Sciences* 43, no. 1–2: 43–49.

Panarese, Paola, and Vittoria Azzarita. 2021. "The Impact of COVID-19 Pandemic on Lifestyle: How Young People Have Adapted Their Leisure and Routine during Lockdown in Italy." *Young* 29 (4_suppl): S35–S64. doi: 10.1177/11033088211031389.

Pandya, Apurvakumar, and Pragya Lodha. 2021. "Social Connectedness, Excessive Screen Time during COVID-19 and Mental Health: A Review of Current Evidence." *Frontiers in Human Dynamics* 3: 1–9. doi: 10.3389/fhumd.2021.684137.

Pieper, Josef. 1998. *Leisure: The Basis of Culture.* South Bend, IN: St. Augustine Press.

Pillay, Jerry. 2020. "COVID-19 Shows the Need to Make Church More Flexible." *Transformation* 37, no. 4: 266–275. doi: 10.1177/0265378820963156.

Plato. 1984. "The Republic." In *Great Dialogues of Plato*, translated by W. H. D. Rouse, 118–422. New York: Mentor Books.

Ramsey, Ramsey Eric. 2011. "On the Dire Necessity of the Useless: Philosophical and Rhetorical Thoughts on Hermeneutics and Education in the Humanities." In *Education, Dialogue, and Hermeneutics*, edited by Paul Fairfield, 92–105. New York: Continuum.

Schiller, Fredrich. 1794/2016. *On the Aesthetic Education of Man.* New York: Penguin Books.

Schrag, Calvin O. 2003. *Communicative Praxis and the Space of Subjectivity.* South Bend, IN: Purdue University Press.

Sheth, Hemai. 2020. "Social Media the Most Preferred Activity During Leisure Time for Native Language Internet Users: Report." The Hindu Business Line, November 11. www.thehindubusinessline.com/info-tech/social-media-the-most

-preferred-activity-during-leisure-time-for-language-first-internet-users-report/article33071859.ece.

Sivan, Atara. 2020. "Reflection on Leisure during COVID-19." *World Leisure Journal* 62, no. 4: 296–99. www.tandfonline.com/doi/full/10.1080/16078055.2020.1825260.

Sparks, Sarah D. 2020. "Five Ideas for a Pandemic-Proof Graduation." *Education Week*. www.edweek.org/teaching-learning/five-ideas-for-a-pandemic-proof-graduation/2020/05.

Tsao, Shu-Feng, Helen Chen, Therese Tisseverasinghe, Yang, and Lainghua Li. 2021. "What Social Media Told Us in the Time of COVID-19: A Scoping Review." *The Lancet: Digital Health* 3, no. 3: E175–E194. doi: 10.1016/S2589-7500(20)30315-0.

Weber, Max. 1905. *The Protestant Ethic and the Spirit of Capitalism*. New York: Pantianos Classics.

Willems, Maartje, and Lona Aalders. 2021. *The Lost Art of Doing Nothing: How the Dutch Unwind with Niksen*. New York: The Experiment.

Wu, Yi-Chi, Ching-Sung Chen, and Yu Juin Chan. 2020. "The Outbreak of COVID-19: An Overview." *Journal of the Chinese Medical Association* 83, no. 3: 217–20.

Chapter 5

COVID-19 at the Nexus of Social Media and Propaganda

Public Health Messaging on Twitter amid Political Polarization

Berrin A. Beasley and Pamela A. Zeiser

Philosopher and ethicist Sissela Bok predicted in her 1999 book *Lying: Moral Choice in Public and Private Life* that a society whose citizens could not tell truthful messages from lies would collapse, but before societal collapse occurred, Bok predicted that "individual choice and survival would be imperiled" (19). Bok's words are troubling in the most peaceful of times because history has shown that propagandistic messaging used for malicious purposes can indeed endanger citizen's lives and a society's survival. One need look no further than Germany's propaganda efforts during World War II to understand the danger of deceptive messaging to life and liberty. It is with these thoughts in mind that we undertook an exploration of selected public health messaging distributed through the Twitter social media platform to determine if the messaging was propagandistic or persuasive. Our concern stemmed from a growing ideological split in the United States regarding COVID-19 and political allegiances, as research has shown one's political alignment typically affected one's perception of the seriousness of the virus and treatments for it (Fratino 2020; Pew Research Center 2019; Rauch 2019). The ability to tell truthful messages from deceptive ones is important to fighting the spread of COVID-19 and for the treatment of it, making it imperative to understand the role of public health messaging during this crisis. While measuring the public's attitude toward COVID-19 messaging is beyond the scope of this chapter, analyzing select COVID-19 public health messaging on social media can help us understand whether these messages could be easily interpreted as truthful or deceptive by the receiver.

We decided for the purposes of this chapter to limit our analysis to messages on the Twitter social media platform because, "Twitter is widely used by journalists and politicians and is where the news gets broken first—attracting others with a strong interest in the news" (Andi 2021). This platform's reputation as a destination for breaking news and information dissemination by politicians, public agencies, public health experts, and journalists makes it the ideal source for people seeking the latest information regarding COVID-19.

Public health messaging has a long history with propaganda, ranging from campaigns to prevent STDs in World War I to ongoing anti-tobacco campaigns in 2020. According to Jowett and O'Donnell (2019), today's public health messaging is more accurately persuasion, because its sources are known, its goals are for the benefit of persuader and persuadee, and change is usually voluntary. Yet as social media amply demonstrates, during the pandemic some people have responded to government COVID-19 messaging as propaganda—as if it were from questionable sources and/or misleading information. A selective and interpretive analysis of public health messages regarding face masks and negative replies to them on Twitter demonstrates that what some users see as useful information and reminders promoting necessary changes for the good of oneself and the community, other users see as lies, oppression, or based upon ulterior motives. This analysis suggests that the factors contributing to negative responses are political polarization, distrust of science, and distrust of or dissatisfaction with governmental actors.

Jowett and O'Donnell (2019) define *propaganda* as "the deliberate, systematic attempt to shape perceptions, manipulate cognitions, and direct behavior to achieve a response that furthers the desired intent of the propagandist" (6). The distinction between *propaganda* and *persuasion*, as presented above, is what information is communicated and who benefits. Both propaganda and persuasion communicate information with the intent to influence people and change behavior. Sources of propaganda may be hidden or visible and the information itself may be true or untrue. The attempt to change behavior benefits the propagandist only. Persuasion, on the other hand, involves accurate, truthful information presented by clearly visible sources. Persuasion is "more mutually satisfying" because both persuader and persuadee benefit. Persuadees undertake voluntary change because they "foresee the fulfillment of a personal or societal need or desire." Persuasion is a reciprocal, transactive process involving interdependency between the persuader and an active audience. Propaganda is manipulative and, in the case of mass audiences, passive. With propaganda, change may be forced and imposed by authorities (Jowett and O'Donnell 2019, p. 31).

With COVID-19, the question of voluntary and mandatory change is complicated for public health messaging surrounding face masking. The U.S.

federal system likely prevents a nationwide mandate, though upon assuming office in 2020 President Joe Biden requested citizens wear masks for 100 days. Government policies at the state and local level have varied and changed over time, with thirty-three states, Washington, DC, and Puerto Rico requiring masks as of March 26, 2021. Other states never imposed mask mandates; in Florida, individual cities had imposed regulations requiring masks but the state government, by executive order of Governor Ron DeSantis, banned any penalties for people refusing to wear them. Ultimately, as Thelwall and Thelwall (2020) point out regarding lockdowns in the United Kingdom, COVID-19 responses may "involve legal enforcement but need widespread partly voluntary compliance to be effective" (947). Public health messaging must convey the reasons for mask mandates, the specific requirements (such as wearing masks at indoor public places vs. outdoor public places), and how to properly wear a mask. "Behaviour change is mandated by the government, but it still relies on the public understanding the message and carrying it out effectively" (Thelwall and Thelwall 2020, p. 947).

Persuasion attempts to influence attitudinal and behavioral change through "shaping" or teaching the public, reinforcing existing attitudes and behaviors, and attempting to outright change behavior. Persuasion builds upon beliefs, values, attitudes, behaviors, and group norms in doing so. "People are reluctant to change," however, and "when situations arise that pose a conflict between national and personal values, people often find it difficult to adapt" (Jowett and O'Donnell 2019, 32, 34).

The conflict between national and personal values is especially problematic for COVID-19 measures such as masking. The pandemic is occurring at the same time as deep political divisions are polarizing American society—meaning there is less consensus on national values for COVID-19 public health messaging to build upon. Much literature exists on the historical antecedents, origins, causes, and impact of polarization, as well as the questions of whether it is driven by elites or voters and how to resolve it. What matters for this study is that partisan polarization exists; Americans are deeply divided over their views of government, national values, and national identities. Today's partisan polarization is also arguably reactionary rather than based on ideology or policy positions: what Republicans stand for, Democrats automatically stand against and vice versa (Rauch 2019). We have perhaps reached the point where policy proposals themselves may be less important than who is making them.

Despite reactionary "us vs. them" behavior, polarization is visible in a number of policy issue areas. The Pew Research Center (2019) reports an average 39 percent gap between Republicans and Democrats across thirty political values including guns, race, immigration, climate change, and the role of government. For example, the question of whether "guns should be more or less available" elicited a difference of 57 percentage points. On political values related to race, that difference was 55 percentage points. Other gaps include climate change (48%), immigration (43%), and role of the government (35%). Pew Research Center's surveys show that partisan differences create the largest divide in American values, more so than differences of "age, race and ethnicity, gender, educational attainment, religious affiliation or other factors" (Pew Research Center 2019).

Although there are also divisions within each party, Pew Research Center's (2019) results allow for generalizations of the two sides of the divide. Republicans are more likely to view illegal immigration and government wastefulness as problems facing America and are less concerned with climate change, racism, and economic inequality. Democrats are the opposite, viewing climate change, racism, economic inequality, and affordable health care as major problems and being less concerned with illegal immigration. Republicans are more likely to see government as usually doing "more harm than good" while Democrats are more likely to see government as often doing a "better job than people give it credit for." Republicans have more confidence in America's ability to solve its problems than Democrats. Both believe the U.S. political and economic systems favor the powerful. The two parties differ on views of race in the United States, with Republicans responding that "white people get few or no advantages in society that black people do not have" while Democrats believe "white people benefit a great deal from advantages that black people do not have." The majority of Republicans believe the country has taken appropriate measures in giving black people equal rights, while the majority of Democrats see the United States as not having "gone far enough when it comes to giving black people equal rights with whites." On the issue of guns, Republicans more likely see existing regulation as "about right" while Democrats favor stricter gun laws (Pew Research Center 2019). These are, of course, simplifications of complex attitudes but they help define the context within which voters see themselves and the other side.

This partisan context affects COVID-19 responses, including masking, just as it affects other public policies. Effective public health messaging—persuasion—must take the audience into account. The audience for COVID-19 messaging is divided not only on political values but also on the value of science. As historian of science Naomi Oreskes points out in a 2020 interview, there remains high trust in science among Americans, but there are "pockets of resistance or scientific rejection that are associated with specific political, economic, or religious demographic groups." Science on COVID-19 is necessarily new and evolving. This fact combines with political and ideological resistance: "people reject scientific advice [about COVID-19] because they see it as the government telling them what to do: 'I don't want the government telling me I have to wear a mask.'" COVID-19 overlaps with "a kind of radical individualism: 'My life is not for someone else to tell me what to do'" (Fratino 2020). Oreskes's pockets of resistance include the ongoing anti-vaccination movement, which also contributes to doubts about COVID-19 science and messaging.

COVID-19 public health messaging, then, necessarily occurs in a larger context of partisan polarization and scientific doubt in the United States. While "simple, clear messaging is a strength," it is also necessary to "tailor messaging to specific audiences" ("How Should We Talk" 2020)—and that is far less simple in a politically polarized environment that, in turn, has polarized views of the coronavirus and measures to prevent it. "Messaging around COVID-19 has tended towards one size fits all" ("How Should We Talk" 2020). Yet previous research on public health messaging has emphasized the need "to recognize and address challenges from groups opposed" to the messages, because "calling attention to public health issues may in some cases activate the opposition" (National Academy 2015). Social media, Twitter specifically, is but one platform through which public health messaging reaches individuals. In this essay, we examine selected COVID-19 public health messages visible on Twitter in 2020 and 2021 and how the messages were likely received by users on both sides of the American political divide.

EXAMINING PUBLIC HEALTH MESSAGING ON TWITTER

For the purpose of this chapter, we conducted a qualitative analysis of selected tweets and replies from 2020 to 2021. Twitter has advantages and disadvantages as a platform for gathering data. In 2021, it had 187 million daily users, was used by 21 percent of Americans, and ranked sixth among social media platforms. Twitter.com is the "9th most visited website globally" (Newberry 2021). Twitter users in the United States are more likely to be under fifty and both wealthier and better educated than the general public. They are also more likely to be Democrats, with 36 percent of users identifying as Democrat and 21 percent as Republican (Wojcik and Hughes 2019). Previous studies have found Twitter users are highly attentive to politics (Ozturkcan et al. 2017; Thelwall and Thelwall 2020) and that the platform can influence public health behavior (Farhadloo et al. 2018). Public health agencies at the international, national, state, and local levels are active on Twitter. #COVID-19 was tied with #BlackLivesMatter for the most used hashtag of 2020. Tweets are in the public domain; our use of them involved no interaction with users and we collected no identifying personal information of individual users. Given continuing ethical debate over the use of direct quotes from users, however, we directly quote only from verified accounts and not from unverified, individual user accounts.

We selected tweets about face masks from the U.S. CDC, White House, and one journalist. We described the original tweets and examined replies to see if and how users responded to the original tweet as persuasion or propaganda. For those that replied negatively, we then moved on to the user profile and timelines to see if we could identify the partisan context within which they placed themselves on Twitter. To do this, we applied frameworks for analysis from the literature above. First, we utilized Jowett and O'Donnell's (2019) three types of response—shaping, reinforcing, and changing—to describe the original tweets (see table 5.1). Second, we used the Pew Research Center data on Republican and Democratic political values to identify Twitter users as one party or the other, based on direct self-descriptions in the profile and/or tweets in their timelines. We also reviewed the timelines for direct and indirect statements in tweets or retweets that indicate support for a party, elected officials, or particular positions on major political issues like guns, immigration, climate change, role of government, and so on. We checked individual user accounts for bots using Botometer, available through the Observatory on Social Media and Network Science Institute at Indiana University. We then categorized the negative responses on both sides of the political divide.

Our goal in identifying the partisan context and interpreting tweeted replies to public health messaging is an exploration of how one person's persuasion is another person's propaganda. When Twitter users react negatively, as if public health messages were propaganda, is that reaction simply partisan or is it more nuanced than that? Does the reaction differ based on type of users posting? Answers to these questions and other results of the analysis provide insight into the nexus between COVID-19 messaging, social media, and perceptions (partisan or not) of persuasion or propaganda.

Table 5.1 Jowett and O'Donnell's Forms of Response to Persuasion

Response Shaping	Response Reinforcing	Response Changing
"Teaching [audience] how to behave and offering positive reinforcement for learning"	"Reminds [audience] about positive attitudes and stimulates them to feel even more strongly by demonstrating their attitudes through specified forms of behavior"	"Involves asking people to switch from one attitude to another . . . to go from a neutral position to a positive or negative one"

Source: Jowett and O'Donnell (2019, p. 32).

ANALYSIS OF PUBLIC HEALTH TWEETS AND REPLIES

Starting with public health agencies or other government entities tweeting about COVID-19, we reviewed one May 8, 2020, tweet from the U.S. Centers for Disease Control (CDC) promoting mask use: "Wear a cloth face covering to help slow the spread of #COVID19. Learn more about these coverings and how you can make one: https://bit.ly/2Ravt42" (CDC 2021). There was also a video using text only to ask and answer the question of whether wearing a mask meant one could stop distancing. The CDC initially discouraged the American public from wearing masks, then revised its advice on April 3, 2020. This tweet comes after that advice and still during the Trump Administration. More replies to this tweet were positive than negative.

We interpret this tweet to exemplify Jowett's and O'Donnell's (2019) response shaping and response reinforcing. This message attempts "to shape the response of an audience by teaching it how to behave and offer[ing] positive reinforcement for learning" (32). For those already convinced by public health messaging on face masks, the tweet also offers the phrase "to help slow the spread of #COVID-19" as an emotional appeal to act for the good of the community (CDC 2020). This reinforces continued mask wearing among those who are compliant, despite the effort it may take due to personal discomfort, mixed messages from politicians, and (in some places) societal pressure against masks.

There were twenty-two users who posted clearly negative replies to the CDC's tweet (some users posted more than one reply). We do not include in that number several users that posted emojis or gifs only, items that could not easily be interpreted as either positive or negative. There were also six hidden replies due to suspended accounts, so we cannot know if they were positive or negative. Of the twenty-two users, three were likely bots based on the use of Botometer. That left nineteen user accounts for us to examine. Based on the Pew Research Center's political values discussed above, we categorize twelve of the users posting negative replies as "Republican" and five as "Democrat." We were unable to determine the political views of one user account. We also separated one user account as undetermined because it expressed extreme conspiracy theories; while we often call these "right-wing" conspiracy theories, we were not comfortable placing such extreme views within the Republican category based on the Pew Research Center values. Five of the Republicans self-identify as such in their profiles or recent tweets, including three who self-identify as Trump or MAGA Republicans in their profile. Two of the five Democrats self-identify as such. Where no self-identification was available, we considered tweets and retweets that were supportive of Republican or Democratic politicians, tweets and retweets that negatively referred to Republican or Democratic politicians, and tweets or retweets that provided clear positions on major issues such as guns, climate change, and so on as discussed above.

Most of the users posting negative replies (seven) determined to be Republicans expressed a distrust of science. One of those expressing distrust of science tied the view to religious beliefs. One that distrusted science also indicated a distrust of Democrats, conflating the two. Another user specifically distrusted the CDC, which could be based on science, politics, or both. The remaining replies included fear of government control/protection of freedoms (two), distrust of the media (one), and concerns about the economy (one). The two undetermined accounts also indicated a distrust of science. Among the five user accounts attributed to Democrats, three distrusted the CDC specifically because of the perceived politicization of the agency under the Trump Administration. One of those also expressed concerns about the economy. The remaining accounts expressed distrust of the media (one) and fear of government control/protection of freedoms (one).

We also reviewed a later CDC tweet about masks, after the Biden Administration was inaugurated. The March 25, 2021, tweet read, "Wearing a mask with multiple layers protects you & others from #COVID19. Do your part to slow the spread" and then listed additional protective measures such as staying 6 feet apart, avoiding crowds, washing hands, and getting a vaccine when available. There was a video as well, explaining how and why masks work (CDC 2021). We interpret this second tweet to also exemplify Jowett's and O'Donnell's response shaping and response reinforcing. The video, specifically, teaches information to users and "do your part to slow the spread" is again an emotional appeal directed toward reinforcement. Because this tweet includes the how and why of mask protection, whereas the first did not, it could potentially also result in response changing. Changing behavior is harder than reinforcing it, as it requires convincing people "to go from a neutral position to a positive" one (Jowett and O'Donnell 2019, 32). The "do your part" appeal can serve as an anchor tying mask wearing to group values and norms, which may theoretically also help convince someone to voluntarily change their behavior.

The responses to this tweet were more numerous and more off-topic, including vaccines, opening schools, mask product advertisements, and so on. There were more bots (11) and there was one parody account (also excluded). There were also more (non-bot) replies indicating conspiratorial beliefs, with one anti-Semitic user blaming COVID-19 on the Jewish community, two tying COVID-19 to the 5G conspiracy, and several opaque religious references conflating COVID-19 and Satan. More replies were off topic than positive or negative; of the on-topic replies, it was about even between positive and negative replies. We again excluded replies that were ambivalent emojis, pictures, or gifs. (Some gifs were clearly negative.) Again, we used the methods noted above to place user accounts on either side of the political divide. Some profile names included their opposition to masks. In the end, we reviewed thirty-six user accounts, of which thirty were Republican, two were Democrats, three were undetermined, and one was a self-identified anarchist. Of the thirty Republican accounts, ten self-identified as Republican, and six of those as Trump or MAGA Republicans. Of the two Democrats, one self-identified as a progressive Democrat. Some of the same categories of replies reoccurred, with fifteen Republicans indicating lack of trust in the CDC (and/or Dr. Anthony Fauci) and eight demonstrating a more general lack of trust in science. One Democrat expressed lack of trust in the CDC, along with two undetermined accounts. One undetermined account indicated distrust in science more generally.

Four Republicans expressed concern about government control, as did one Democrat, one anarchist, and one undetermined account. Two Republicans indicated religious opposition to wearing masks and one Republican's reply indicated a belief that the entire pandemic was a conspiracy. There were no responses related directly to distrust of Democrats, distrust of the media, or responses to economic concerns surrounding the pandemic. (There was one bot-generated response that mask wearing was about making money, not health.)

While there may be many reasons for distrust of the CDC, a number of replies to the May 8, 2020, tweet and many more replies to the March 25, 2021, CDC tweet highlighted contradictions between early and later CDC recommendations and/or indicated refusal to believe current recommendations based on the fact the CDC changed its stance on mask wearing. The evolving science of, knowledge of, and responses to COVID-19 led to such changes, but for users who resist or doubt science, this becomes further evidence that science is wrong at best and untruthful at worst. For others, it may simply be confusing or contradictory. This finding tracks with Benham et al. (2020), who found in focus group interviews in Canada that inconsistent or mixed COVID-19 messaging was the largest source of complaint against public health measures.

Moving from the CDC to the Biden White House, a January 23, 2020, tweet stated, "Please wear a mask" and included a video from Dr. Anthony Fauci demonstrating how to correctly wear one (White House 2020). The tweet itself fits Jowett's and O'Donnell's (2019) response reinforcing; it is a simple statement, and the use of the word "please" can constitute an emotional appeal. For those who view the video of Dr. Fauci, that part of the tweet is response shaping as it demonstrates proper mask use. For fans of Dr. Fauci, the video may also be response reinforcing.

The vast majority of replies to this tweet were positive. There were off-topic tweets about vaccines, police brutality, marijuana, and Bernie memes.

We continue to exclude replies that are ambivalent emojis, pictures, gifs, or only the word "no" (or more profane versions of that word). We found only one bot among the negative replies and there were at least two negative replies from other countries (also excluded). We reviewed twenty-nine user accounts posting negative replies. We identified sixteen accounts as Republican, five of which self-identified and two of those as Trump or MAGA Republicans. There were four Democrats, five undetermined, one self-identified anarchist, and one self-identified Libertarian. The most common negative reply was new and criticized either President Biden or Dr. Fauci for failing to wear masks themselves, often including pictures of them mask-less from press conferences. (Explanations for this include distancing between politicians and reporters, effective communication, and accessibility for the hearing impaired.) One Democrat, the anarchist, and two undetermined users also posted comments accusing the two of hypocrisy. The anarchist also indicated concerns about government control/protection of freedoms, as did three Republican and one undetermined user. The second-most common negative reply expressed distrust of science in general or Dr. Fauci in particular. There were six Republican replies of this type, along with one Democrat, two undetermined, and one Libertarian. Another new negative response, made by two Democrats, expressed "COVID fatigue" in general or specifically regarding mask wearing.

The White House tweet fell in between the timing of the two CDC tweets and that may explain fewer bots; by March 2021 there was not only more time for but also potentially more COVID-19 fatigue-related dissatisfaction leading to the creation and/or targeting of bot accounts toward COVID-19 public health messaging. It makes sense that the White House account would be followed by more international user accounts than the CDC, given the profile of the U.S. presidency. As well as the two negative replies from outside the United States, there were at least half a dozen positive replies made by international user accounts as well.

Journalist, editorial writer, and self-described progressive Nicholas Kristof adds his call for wearing masks to those of government entities. In a July 1, 2020, tweet, Kristof tweets the main point of his *New York Times* opinion piece, the link to it, and invites conversation: "My new column, just posted online: 'Refusing to Wear a Mask Is Like Driving Drunk.' Trump and the GOP emphasize personal responsibility. This is the time to show some, and call on all Americans to wear masks. https://nyti.ms/31HN7C2 Thoughts?" (Kristoff 2020). This tweet is reinforcing for those who disliked Trump and were mask compliant—in comparing the refusal to wear masks with drunk driving, it turns mask wearing into a virtue. The full editorial includes facts that could shape user responses. The tweet illustrates Jowett's and O'Donnell's (2019) idea of an anchor, which is something "already accepted by the persuadee." To convince people to change, "the persuader has to relate the change to something in which the persuadee already believes" (32). Drunk driving is such an anchor as well as a subject of ongoing public health campaigns. The use of this anchor gives the tweet the possibility that it could change behavior. The tweet could also be seen as daring Republicans to live up to their political values of personal responsibility, which could lead to response changing—or, perhaps, reinforcement of anti-mask feelings among Republicans if they perceive the tone of the tweet and full editorial to be condescending or patronizing. This tweet also demonstrates the point that little public health messaging occurs only on Twitter; government and other actors emphasize mask wearing through many types of media, traditional, new, and social. Kristof's editorial is traditional and social media provides him with an additional way to advertise it.

The majority of responses to this tweet were positive, logically anticipated on a platform that includes more users identifying as Democrats. There were few negative replies, with only five. This was surprising, as one could expect a prominent, progressive journalist to attract naysayers; on the other hand, conservatives could simply choose not to follow him. Four negative replies were from Republicans (one self-identified) and one undetermined. One Republican and the undetermined account expressed concerns about government control/protection of freedoms, two Republicans indicated distrust of science and one Republican communicated distrust of the media. There were no negative replies from Democrats and no new reasons given for negative replies. Beyond social media, there was negative response to Kristof's column published in the Pittsburgh Post-Gazette's Letters to the Editor. Fonzie (2020) turned Kristof's complaint of American passivity among those not wearing masks into an argument that those who do wear masks are passive citizens—presumably demonstrating his concern over government control.

ONE PERSON'S PERSUASION IS ANOTHER PERSON'S PROPAGANDA

This selective review of COVID-19 public health messaging tweets and replies indicates there is a partisan divide on the acceptance of science in general. Distrust of the CDC, specifically, also appears partisan, especially because in March 2020 Democrats who distrusted the CDC clearly expressed suspicion of the organization under the Trump Administration. In March 2021, however, it was primarily Republicans who distrusted the CDC. The perceived hypocrisy of politicians for not wearing masks was also primarily partisan. Small partisan deviations for these categories of replies are not surprising, given divisions within as well as between parties. Fear of government control crosses the partisan divide, as does distrust of the media and concerns about the economy. It is interesting that replies expressing concerns about the economy did not increase or even reappear in the most recent tweets reviewed. Where negative Twitter replies indicate one person's persuasion is another person's propaganda, the larger U.S. context of political polarization and distrust of science helps explain them. Both of those factors contribute to distrust of or dissatisfaction with government entities such as the U.S. CDC or White House.

An understanding of the context for and partisan reactions to public health messaging can enable those who craft the messages to better design and target the messages. The partisan differences found in this review of tweets and responses reinforce that for COVID-19 "there's no monolithic audience out there." The "need to frame the message differently for different groups of people" competes with a need "to be consistent with the fact and the outcomes you want to achieve" (Marquez 2020). At the same time, however, the results of this analysis show that distrust of the CDC combined with a more general distrust of science creates resistance to evolving information and public health measures. The complexity of overlap between polarization, distrust of science, and distrust of government highlights Uttara Bharath Kumar's recommendation that public health messengers acknowledge "where they were wrong before because that was the best available information at the time" ("How Should We Talk" 2020). Responses to tweets about mask wearing reviewed here indicate that many users—often Republicans—either have not received or accepted that message. While Twitter users may be more Democratic, targeted messaging on the platform could better speak to minority Republicans.

Now that we've discussed our findings on the potential perception of public health messages as truthful or deceptive on Twitter, it's time to circle back to our impetus for this chapter, whether Bok's assertion that the inability of message receivers to determine whether messages are truthful or deceptive would lead to societal collapse, or prior to collapse, that individual choice and survival would be imperiled. Our analysis revealed that in the United States, one's political alignment likely affected one's trust in Twitter public health messaging regarding COVID-19, regardless of whether the message itself technically met Jowell and O'Donnell's (2019) definition of persuasion as opposed to propaganda. The potential influence of political ideology on message interpretation can be compared to COVID-19 death rates as an example of how this inability to discern truthful messages from lies imperiled individual choice and survival. Findings by the Pew Research Center indicate,

> Overall, the COVID-19 death rate in *all* counties Trump won in 2020 is substantially higher than it is in counties Biden won (as of the end of February 2022,

326 per 100,000 in Trump counties and 258 per 100,000 in Biden counties). (Jones 2022; emphasis in original)

These findings take into account that at the beginning of COVID-19, when Trump was in office, more deaths occurred in the Northeast, which tended to vote Democrat. However, as the pandemic progressed, Biden was sworn in as president, and COVID-19 vaccinations became widely available, the geographic locations with the most deaths were areas that voted heavily Republican (Jones 2022). This geographic shift in COVID-19 deaths correlates with political affiliation and voting behaviors. Could the ability to discern truth from lies in public health messaging have prevented some of these later COVID-19 deaths, regardless of political party affiliation, or does political affiliation negatively affect one's ability to discern the truthfulness or deceitfulness of public health messaging?

Some of the answers to these questions lie in the foundation of public messaging disbelief built by political party leaders and social media influencers. When the people who head one's political party tell you messages from the opposing political party or parties are lies, do you believe those people? Should you believe those people? What about social media influencers who peddle misinformation or disinformation? What responsibility do they bear in laying the foundation of public messaging disbelief? Communication ethicists Englehardt and Barney (2002) write that reason must be employed to justify beliefs and actions, both individually and societally. "Ethicists generally hold that while reason is not the only guide to truth, it provides the best direction," (8). We propose that while society plays an important part in preparing citizens for applying critical thinking skills to any type of communication, it is ultimately the responsibility of individuals to use reason as a guide to truth, including when evaluating social media posts related to COVID-19, whether these posts are made by public health professionals, political party leaders, journalists, family members, friends, or social media influencers. Ideally, individuals and society would work interactively in preparing for and undertaking reasoned analysis—of social media or any other form of communication. This interaction occurs through an admittedly complex blend of education, political culture, leadership, values, and accountability based on the responsibility that individuals have to contribute to a society that is founded on reason.

This is a call to action on the part of all individuals to learn from the past as they take responsibility for their future health. What we have discovered from our analysis of COVID-19 public health messaging posted on Twitter and political polarization, in conjuction with COVID-19 death data in the United States, leads us to suggest that one way to reduce loss of life to the coronavirus or future public health pandemics is for all individuals to engage in a reasoned analysis of public health information provided on social media and elsewhere. By employing Jowett and O'Donnell's (2019) definitions of persuasion and propaganda when analyzing public health messaging on social media, individuals can engage in a reasoned approach to truth by asking: Is the information truthful? Is the source of the information hidden or visible? Is the information manipulative? Who benefits from this information? As Jowett and O'Donnell (2019) explain, propaganda is manipulative and benefits only the propagandist. Persuasion involves accurate, truthful information presented by clearly visible sources that is mutually satisfying to the persuader and the persuadee (31). Persuasive information about a public health crisis will never be deceitful, but propaganda about a public health crisis will be, and without a reasoned approach to information processing, some people may mistake propaganda for persuasion or persuasion for propaganda—and it could cost them their lives.

REFERENCES

Andi, Simgi. 2021. "How and Why Do Consumers Access News on Social Media?" *Reuters Institute for the Study of Journalism,* June 23. https://reutersinstitute.politics.ox.ac.uk/digital-news-report/2021/how-and-why-do-consumers-access-news-social-media.

Benham, Jamie L., Raynell Lang, Katharina Kovacs Burns, Gail MacKean, Tova Léveillé, Brandi McCormack, Hasan Sheikh, Madison M. Fullerton, Theresa Tang, Jean-Christophe Boucher, et al. 2021. "Attitudes, Current Behaviours and Barriers to Public Health Measures That Reduce COVID-19 Transmission: A Qualitative Study to Inform Public Health Messaging." *PloS One* 16, (2): e0246941. doi: 10.1371/journal.pone.0246941.

Bok, Sissela. 1999. *Lying: Moral Choice in Public and Private Life.* New York: Vintage Books.

CDC (@CDCgov). 2020. "Wear a cloth face covering to help slow the spread of #COVID19. Learn more about these coverings and how you. . . ." Twitter post, May 8. https://twitter.com/CDCgov/status/1258779943707774976.

CDC (@CDCgov). 2021. "Wearing a mask with multiple layers protects you & others from #COVID19. Do your part to slow the spread." Twitter post, March 25. https://twitter.com/CDCgov/status/1375193774205235202.

Desmon, Stephanie. 2020. "How Should We Talk about COVID-19?" *Johns Hopkins Center for Communication Programs,* September 28. https://ccp.jhu.edu/2020/09/28/communication-covid19-uttara/?gclid=EAIaIQobChMI6ZWWuaDY7wIVAYTICh0rxgWiEAMYASAAEgIShPD_BwE.

Englehardt, Elaine E., and Ralph D. Barney. 2002. *Media Ethics: Principles for Moral Decisions.* Chicago, IL: Thomson Learning.

Farhadloo, Mohsen, Kenneth Winneg, Man-Pui Sally Chan, Kathleen Hall Jamieson, and Dolores Albarracin. 2018. "Associations of Topics of Discussion on Twitter with Survey Measures of Attitudes, Knowledge, and Behaviors Related to Zika: Probabilistic Study in the United States." *JMIR Public Health and Surveillance* 4, (1) 57–67. doi: 10.2196/publichealth.8186.

Finizio, Vincent. 2020. "Odd Comparison." *Pittsburgh Post-Gazette*, July 15. www.post-gazette.com/opinion/letters/2020/07/15/Odd-comparison/stories/202007150039.

Fratino, Antonella. 2020. "Naomi Oreskes on the Science of Climate Change and COVID-19—and Those Who Deny It." *McGill Reporter*, September 15. https://reporter.mcgill.ca/naomi-oreskes-on-the-science-of-climate-change-and-covid-19-and-those-who-deny-it.

Jones, Bradley. 2022. "The Changing Political Geography of COVID-19 over the Last Two Years." *Pew Research Center*, March 3. www.pewresearch.org/politics/2022/03/03/the-changing-political-geography-of-covid-19-over-the-last-two-years.

Jowett, Garth S., and Victoria O'Donnell. 2019. *Propaganda & Persuasion*. 7th ed. Newbury Park, CA: SAGE.

Marquez, Jennifer Rainey. 2020. "A Failure to Communicate." *Georgia State University Research Magazine*. https://news.gsu.edu/research-magazine/a-failure-to-communicate-covid-19-pandemic-public-health-messaging.

Newberry, Claire. "36 Twitter Stats All Marketers Need to Know in 2021." *Hootsuite*, February 3. https://blog.hootsuite.com/twitter-statistics.

Nicholas Kristof (@NickKristof). 2020. "My new column, just posted online: 'Refusing to Wear a Mask Is Like Driving Drunk.' Trump and the GOP emphasize. . . ." Twitter post, July 1. https://twitter.com/NickKristof/status/1278471719251042305.

Ozturkcan, Selcen, Nihat Kasap, Muge Cevik, and Tauhid Zaman. 2017. "An Analysis of the Gezi Park Social Movement Tweets." *Aslib Journal of Information Management* 69, no. 4: 426–40.

Pew Research Center. 2019. "In a Politically Polarized Era, Sharp Divides in Both Partisan Coalitions: Partisanship Remains Biggest Factor in Public's Political Values." *Pew Research Center*, December 17. www.pewresearch.org/politics/2019/12/17/in-a-politically-polarized-era-sharp-divides-in-both-partisan-coalitions.

Rauch, Jonathan. 2019. "Rethinking Polarization." *National Affairs* 41: 86–100.

Thelwall, Mike, and Saheeda Thelwall. 2020. "A Thematic Analysis of Highly Retweeted Early COVID-19 Tweets: Consensus, Information, Dissent, and Lockdown Life." *Aslib Journal of Information Management* 72, no. 6: 945–62. doi:10.1108/AJIM-05-2020-0134.

White House (@WhiteHouse). 2021. "Please wear a mask." Twitter post, January 23. https://twitter.com/WhiteHouse/status/1353111551696375808.

Wojcik, Stephan, and Adam Hughes. 2019. "Sizing Up Twitter Users." *Pew Research Center*, April 24. www.pewresearch.org/internet/2019/04/24/sizing-up-twitter-users.

Chapter 6

Divisiveness, Meaningful Lives, and the Hope of Compassion

Social Media in the Time of COVID-19

Mitchell R. Haney

In early July of 2020, an Arizona woman walked into her local Target and videoed herself violently clearing shelves of facemasks while engaging in a profane tirade over pandemic restrictions. Subsequently, she uploaded this video to Instagram. Prior to the pandemic, she had run her own marketing company with notable clients, had an active social life with friends, and was an active member in health and wellness communities. She had even purchased N95 masks earlier in the pandemic. After the video went viral, she was given the moniker of "QAnon Karen" (Collins 2020).

The phenomenon of that friend or loved one who changed "overnight" after exposure to some new interpretation of the world is not new as a result of the pandemic or even the advent of the internet. The phenomena of such radical transformations are not new at all—they are a staple of religious conversion, self-help movements, and to some extent, psychological therapy for much of the past two centuries and even earlier in the case of religion. In fact, people make decisions and plot bold new trajectories in their lives all the time. So, why do these particular transformations—in this social-historical context of global, electronic interconnectedness—strike us as unsettling? And how should we respond to them in others? A broad ethical issue that has always intrigued me is how should we approach people seeking to be authentic to themselves (especially in ways that appear to be distinct from their past) in a world in which much is outside of their control and when we all have epistemic blind spots that cannot be easily or, sometimes, ever corrected? Exploration of such questions within our technological context during the pandemic will unfold below.

PANDEMIC ISOLATION, SOCIAL MEDIA, AND APPLIED ETHICS

Due to pandemic lockdowns or even self-isolation, there has been a significant increase in the use of virtual communications and reliance on the digital communities found in social media. In the first wave of the virus, there was a 61 percent increase in the use of social media as people were under lockdown in the attempt to prevent the spread of COVID-19 (Kantar 2020). The evidence is that we turned to a greater use of electronically mediated communication overall to replace face-to-face interaction during the pandemic. The Pew Research Center found, in the spring of 2021, that 90 percent of those they polled said that the internet was, at least, important to them personally during the pandemic, and 58 percent said it was "essential." This was a rise of 5 percent over a year earlier when the pandemic was already in full swing (McClain et al. 2021).

Social media may be a handy means to mitigate loneliness brought on by physical isolation, and a means to connect to others who we aren't already isolated with at home. Thus, social media allowed friendships and extended family connections to be maintained. We are generally social beings, after all. During COVID-19 people made new friends and started new relationships via social media; they reconnected with old friends and family or even discovered and connected with new family. For example, during the first wave of COVID-19, Ancestry.com saw a 37 percent increase in new subscriptions (CBS Miami 2020). Although many people may admit that social media connections are an inferior substitute to face-to-face interactions, they likely admit it has been better than no contact at all or the continual interactions with the same limited number of people, every day, in the same space. (Just ask parents who didn't get a reprieve from their kids as they did distance learning and they were no longer were able to visit their own friends regularly for adult conversations.) Social media and the internet, in addition, have provided a nearly immediate, real-time connection to happenings in the "outside world" which had become a more threatening space. The immediacy of information was heightened by the ubiquity of the smart phone because individuals needn't jockey for control over more communal forms of technology, such as TVs or computers, to have access to sources of information available on the internet. I have experienced many of these benefits, and I have heard as much from many others during the pandemic. I assume that many of you reading this will relate. However, there have certainly been concerns.

We have come to know of virtual meeting fatigue ("Zoom Burnout"), increased anxiety and depression, the cascade of misinformation or simple information overload, inequality exacerbated by the digital divide, echo chambers, and the increased divisions within communities to name only a few of the maladies that seem to be related to increased usage of the internet and social media during the pandemic. The pandemic did not cause such concerns, as is obvious, because they were already issues raised about the internet and social media before we had a worldwide lockdown. However, the turn to a greater reliance on or use of these communication tools as a result of the pandemic may be exacerbating the issues to which the usage and function of the internet as well as social media had already been playing some role. What can a philosophical eye, however, bring to such a set of social entanglements?

A prominent ethical approach to the problematic effects of social media would be concerned with prescribing philosophically justified moral rules or policies regulating the functioning of the technology through such things as the way social media platforms operate, the use of algorithms, the use or the access to the internet and social media by users, and so on. There is certainly an importance to thinking as a civic body about the internet and social media in the same way we might establish ethical rules with regards to limiting behavior in other realms of civil society. Take for instance, markets. In a generally free society, members of society decide through some governmental system of representation what goods and services may be traded in a market and what may not. In addition, for those goods and services we allow, we may set rules about how they may be marketed and to whom. Civil society, in addition, decides whether and how to remove bad actors from the market, and society can change the rules to fit innovations in goods and services, as well as to react to increased understanding of health, safety, and other impacts of goods and services. Such market regulations often reflect moral or ethical standards rather than just efficiency and other pragmatic goals of the markets. Such rules can become very fine-grained, and this setting of limits can even move into the private sector. Some businesses have now appointed ethicists in their firms to lead ethical thinking and rules governing particular features of their services. Business ethics, as an area of applied ethics, often hope to help civil society evaluate which policy choices would be morally best in that limited sphere.

The point is that a major trajectory of philosophical applied ethics, if not the dominant one, has been to be a handmaiden of policy in given domains of human interaction. Applied ethics often aims to give moral guidance on social rules and policies. However, discerning a list of rules or guidelines governing social media use is not my concern here, but what I will discuss will still broadly intersect with general public welfare. In fact, it will intersect with central issues for liberalism in a pluralistic society: How ought we balance individual freedom and the public good, or how do we deal with conflicts between competing individual conceptions of good in a world that respects pluralism?

The aim of thinking about ethical issues to determine the best rules or policies for social good within the concrete circumstances of some domain has, I think, tended to eclipse perspectives around living lives with individual meaning and value. It is not that applied ethics has been entirely silent on such issues, but in the context of European liberalism, which in general tries to be neutral on the matter of individual good, applied ethics has tended to focus on matters of determining right and wrong behavior. European liberalism has dedicated itself to allowing people the freedom to choose their own conception of the good life and a way to do that is to remain largely impartial or silent about the good life. Nonetheless, applied ethics and liberal society in general can only remain silent or impartial concerning individual good and focused on refereeing behavior for so long. The simple dictum of your liberty ends where mine begins or relying on the Harm Principle—one may act as one wishes unless one's actions pose a clear and present danger of harm to others—seem much too thin to really grapple with the realities involved in people seeking meaningful lives in proximity to one another based in divergent axiological realities.

The general idea is that people take on personal projects about which they place significant importance. It is how we generate meaningful lives. However, our projects may have deleterious effects (direct or indirect) on others (or on ourselves) and our projects may be deeply incompatible with the projects with whom we share our world. There is only so much that reflective social groups can do in framing rules, a priori, that prescribe moral limits on peoples' behavior or to prevent conflict. At some point, we must think about the value contents and even why people find the content of their projects so essential to their lives.

We regularly see it stated how divisive our society has become, but not much is said about what to do given this state of affairs. It is often merely stated as a lamentable fact about our present time. A recurrent example is the seeming, widening influence of conflictual worldviews. One of the most highlighted conflicts comes from the apparent wider acceptance of those things that have been baptized as "conspiracy theories." These worldviews appear to have gained greater acceptance during the pandemic—although this has also been reasonably disputed (Uscinsky 2021). "QAnon Karen" (from the opening of this chapter) is but one concrete example of a person who is acting on values and beliefs (a worldview or perspective) as part of a project to which she became devoted and that gave her life new purpose or meaning during the pandemic.

I wholeheartedly believe that people can be captured by a wide range of worldviews (they can be good, benign, questionable, or evil) and people's commitments to the projects that follow from their worldviews can and do create interpersonal tension or conflict. Commitment to our projects leaves us all open to experiencing discord and divisiveness with others. Much of what I would like to do in this essay is a rendering of this complex phenomenon in this particular sociohistorical moment, to motivate why such a rendering can help to illuminate the project of personal well-being, as well as motivate certain pragmatic resources for living well together in a liberal, pluralistic society where the contents of our projects leave us vulnerable to conflict. And this illumination, I hope, will help us see approaches to interpersonal division that need not assume that we need to seek some a priori rules for determining future limits on personal liberty. In doing so, I hope to address my opening interests in how we may best ethically respond to others who, in seeking authentic and meaningful lives, commit to projects that become a source of conflict with those in their lives. In particular, I am interested in cases where persons have latched on to new projects, apparently divergent from their former selves, and about where these new projects are a source interpersonal divisiveness with those whom they previously had little disagreement. In short, how might a particular philosophical approach help us address divisiveness in the present cultural milieu?

MEANING, PROJECTS, AND LUCK

Bernard Williams (1981a, 1985) urges us to reflect seriously upon the role and value of peoples' personal projects and the meaning or value of such in considering broader questions of ethics (see Smart and Williams 1973). This is a theme that had been lost, he seems to urge, in European liberalism's value neutrality and the subsequent necessary focus on just arbitrating behavior. It is not that Williams or others who are interested in reviving an interest in such "personal values" desire to trample individual liberty, but they do think that when such an important element of valuable living was circumscribed from philosophical investigation or critique, in the name of liberty, that this was in fact a disservice to liberty. In Apollonian fashion, we cannot be free, if we do not know ourselves (at least to whatever extent that is possible).

While it may be methodologically useful to demarcate the value of actions from what it is to be a good person, from what is to be living a good or meaningful life, the conceptual demarcations are not an indication that there is or ought to be a genuine divide between axiological realms when we make an all-things-considered assessment of what kind of life is worth living. In this context, Williams (1985) raises the issue that modern ethics had given a backseat to the question of a personally meaningful life, or the value of personal projects, in order to focus on understanding what actions are permissible, obligatory, and forbidden, as well as to simply figuring out rules for adjudicating conflicts when our actions impede others' freedom. Modern ethics had become more about the ethics of discrete public obligations, and less about questions concerning what constitutes a life well-lived for complex individuals living in relationship with each other (174ff). Individuals were allowed to become thin and depthless in the name of their personal freedom. Persons were to be viewed formally as rights-bearers or self-interest maximizers, and we should not try to value or evaluate others' conception of the good. Such questions are private, and they need not concern the ethicist. However, it should be noted that Williams (1981c) raises concerns about such a form of privacy when he argues that our personal projects make up our character over time, and character is a public display of our commitments, choices, and so on, through patterns of behavior. Thus, it should be no surprise that delving into understandings of personal good leads to questions of how we should get along with one another in the public space, and vice versa, because such personal good is intimately connected to a public character. To think that we can cleanly isolate and insolate these normative realms, of private good and public action, a priori is, at best, a kind of philosophical tool and, at worst, a philosophical delusion. The concern I will outline below is that this view of privacy and public neutrality about the good hides from view fruitful ethical approaches to dealing with those persons who embark on life projects that can be disruptive to themselves and others.

Williams (1981b), in his influential essay "On Moral Luck," might first appear to be an odd place to start an ethical discussion of individuals' search for meaning and social media, but it is an essay of rich resource. Although the essay launched a bit of a cottage philosophical industry around moral responsibility and issues of good or bad luck (and discerning types of luck), it also ties into a theme that recurs in much of Williams's work on ethics concerning the value of individuals' personal commitments (23–26). The way the essay ties into his concerns with personal commitments does so with an example that I believe is fruitful for thinking about the kinds of cases we are perplexed by these days, cases of people who have come to commit themselves to projects that put them in sudden discord with others.

William's (1981b) essay opens a query around a topic of whether or not one can be held in judgment (praised or blamed) for actions and their consequences, if any part of this was outside one's control. He considers a case of a fictional Gauguin who comes to believe that to be a great painter he must move to Tahiti and abandon his obligations and relationships in France in the process. The case hinges on Gauguin's pursuit, which has great meaning to him, and this is often forgotten in the discussion as it isn't essential to the question about luck per se, but it is reflective of William's (1973, 1981c, 1981d, 1985) recurrent concern about the value of personal projects. To continue, Williams (1981c) asks us to consider the fact that whether or not Gauguin succeeds in becoming a great painter is not something Gauguin could know ahead of time, and many factors would have to contribute to it—or at least not impede it. For instance, he would have to survive the voyage from France and remain in good enough health to paint. He would have to have access to proper painting supplies once in Tahiti, as well as still have access to authoritative art circles able to judge his work on its merits, and so on. These various elements of success are entirely out of Gauguin's hands, but they are each entirely relevant to the success or failure of his project. And his success or failure ultimately will ground our judgment of his life choice. For Williams (1981c), whether or not we judge this fictional Gauguin to have made a reasonable, even if radical, life choice, based on what he takes to be a meaningful project, appears to depend on whether or not he succeeded in becoming a great painter. In addition, his success or failure was in significant ways beyond his control (23).

If we correctly judge people as having been reasonable, ethical, or correct, and so on in their life choices, it does matter whether or not they succeeded in some important way (or, at the very least, they did not fail). And, if people lack significant control over whether or not they ultimately succeed, then this is a matter of what Williams calls, "moral luck." In the literature on moral luck, this type of luck is now referred to as "resultant luck." There are other types of moral luck that have subsequently been discussed, but they need not concern us here. I will note that there are critics who argue that we are simply incorrect in making judgments in cases where resultant luck is involved. For instance, they may say we can only judge Gauguin's intentions since that is all he can actually control. This may seem like a reasonable and tolerant view, but it may be too tolerant. For instance, as we may say, the road to hell can be paved with good intentions. We do reasonably blame people for well-meaning but failed actions. This is especially true in cases where success seemed improbable. But we also blame people for failing to succeed in cases of probable success, and their intent or positive attitude may make little difference to our judgment. We also praise successes often without knowledge of intent. Thus, our practice and phenomenology seem to defy reduction to simple, intentional-based models. What our practices of passing judgment indicate is that conflicts between people often arise within the scope of personal projects and the actions that flow from them in a world that is permeated with resultant luck.

Let me add a twist to Williams's fictional Gauguin to make his case closer to cases that we see troubling us today. Suppose Gauguin had a hobby of drawing and painting and had some talent, but he never felt he had a calling. He occasionally gifted works to friends and family, which they adored, and they believed he had natural talent, but nothing more. He also found meaning in other activities that supported his family, close friends, and giving back to his community. He then discovered in the back of a magazine an "art test" that asked interested readers to copy a drawing of a Tahitian woman and to mail their copy in to the art school for evaluation. He sent in his own rendering out of curiosity. They responded and said to him, "You have great talent! You should join us in Tahiti. You could be a part of the growing *Paris of the South Pacific!*" This communication suddenly rearranged Gauguin's life goals and gave him an utterly new direction in life. His wife, extended family, and friends no longer psychologically recognize him. He is now "Test Gauguin," and his concerns are singularly focused on becoming a great artist and being a part of a movement to make the poor Polynesian islands attain the stature of their French colonizer. Despite "Test Gauguin's" friends' and family's protestations and bewilderment, he heads off to Tahiti to be an artist and finds great meaning in this project—he has a new purpose. Note, "Test Gauguin's" project is still subject to the same resultant luck highlighted in Williams's original thought experiment. First, I think this twist on William's example begins to parallel something closer to the rearrangement of a life plan discovered through social media that we see today with the internet. Second, I think it begins to demonstrate that resultant luck is *prima facie* true in virtue of our lived experience as people, judges, and social practitioners. We judge ourselves and others not only by intentions but also in the face of success or failure (even in the face of conditions that we do not entirely control). "Test Gauguin" will likely be judged not solely on the basis of his intentions, but whether or not he actually succeeds in this endeavor.

Williams's (1981c) example, and the permutation thereof, also raises related issues worth exploring. What is the value of people pursuing their own projects under the conditions where they lack control? How should we treat people in the grasp of their own projects, especially those about which we either disagree or which we don't quite comprehend, and which we also do not yet know the outcome? Or even those projects which we have good reason to believe will fail, but the person engaged in the project believes otherwise? In short, what role should we take when others are pursuing their own life projects (making their own meaningful lives) in a world where there is contingency, neither they nor us are omnipotent, and the results are not yet known (resultant luck is either still unsettled or the person whose project it fails to accept, even the probable results)?

Let us consider two hypothetical people even closer to our state of affairs—Ron and Rhonda. They each were avid supporters of Bernie Sanders in 2016. They were taken by his message that the economic elite supported members of both parties and that through their financial power the elite essentially controlled American policy to the disadvantage of working-class people such as themselves. They each believed the United States needed a leader that would bring substantial reforms to the political system to "remove money from politics." They each had good high school educations and some college, and they each had gone on and been successful mastering trades. They each worked hard, but that essentially maintained an adequate standard of living rather than advanced them any further economically, and each of them had also experienced times of frightful precarity. Ron and Rhonda had also witnessed numerous friends easily fall through economic cracks due to no fault of their own. Well-paying jobs were lost due to outsourcing and downsizing, and small, private businesses were put out of business due to encroachment from "big-box" competitors without any local ties. During the 2015–2016 primaries, Ron and Rhonda each volunteered for the Bernie campaign in their local areas. They canvassed on his behalf, made phone calls, and so on, and they each would enthusiastically travel to his rallies anytime he was near their hometowns. Ron and Rhonda were each seriously disappointed when he lost the nomination, and they were each furious when it appeared that the Democratic National Committee (DNC) had not been impartial, and it seemed they had "tipped-the-scale" to undermine Sanders. This later news reinforced his message that corporate elites ran both parties to maintain the status quo. When Sanders decided not to fight it at the convention and backed Hillary Clinton as the nominee, Ron and Rhonda were deeply disenchanted and felt abandoned.

Ron and Rhonda were, like many Americans, regular users of the internet and social media. This was a technology that Sanders, following Obama, had masterfully harnessed to get out his message, organize, and raise campaign funds. It is where they had each latched onto Bernie's anti-establishment message. They continued on with their lives after the election, but due to their disappointment and anger over the state of the nation they continued to follow politics still hoping to make sense of Bernie's defeat and acquiescence. Seeking insight, Ron and Rhonda continued to read articles shared by their fellow Bernie supporters that they had worked alongside. All along, social media algorithms each were continuously building digital profiles of their interests and their likely internet behavior. The pandemic comes along, their work is shut down or moved online, and their presence on social media and, along with it, their data profile increase quite a bit. What kinds of content and prompts would keep Ron and Rhonda coming back and staying even longer? They both had a penchant to click and like articles that were wary of capitalism, corporations, and government; articles which explained that behind the scenes were deeper forces at work; and articles that had a call for resistance to the status quo. However, Ron and Rhonda's online activity were each creating distinct online data profiles the more they utilized social media. Ron, always concerned about his health, tended to read more articles that were wary of science, joined natural health groups, and watched more videos about natural health remedies. Rhonda, on the other hand, read more pro-labor articles, including those related to international worker solidarity, and she joined a few private leftwing political groups, but she also enjoyed watching marksmanship and hunting videos because she was raised in an outdoors, shooting-sports family.

Ron and Rhonda are stuck at home under COVID-19 and spending more time on social media. They are being sent recommendations for websites, articles, or new persons to connect with that they hadn't noticed before. Each have one or more that pique their interest, because of shared concerns, and these websites, articles, or persons seemed to promise something that they seemed to be missing. An answer? Something new to fill the time?

Ron is led to a person or information that tells him that the Democrats are among a wealthy group of elites that run, among other things, a child sex-trafficking ring in Washington, DC, and above all things, Clinton needed to win to keep that hidden. In addition, they are saying that COVID-19 is a hoax being used to control us, and it is no more dangerous than the common flu. However, Donald Trump is here to expose such fraud, the heinous acts of violence, drain the swamp, and bring justice to these vile people. He becomes "QAnon Ron," who watches hours of QAnon YouTube videos, watches for Qdrops and "Baker" videos with bated breath, regularly attends anti-lockdown and Pro-Trump rallies in his region, and, ultimately, he was proudly in Washington, DC, on January 6th to protect his country and his president (although he never assaulted anyone nor entered the Capitol building). He may still believe that COVID-19 is a hoax, vaccines are a means to track the citizenry, the election was stolen, and Trump will make a triumphant return to eliminate evildoers and save America. In his mind, he will do what is necessary (including violent resistance) to aid Trump in this endeavor.

Rhonda, due to her data profile, is led to a person, video, or website for her local chapter of the John Brown Gun Club. Here she finds a community of like-minded leftists who are very wary of corporations and government, who want to protect minorities and the working class, but still believe in the Second Amendment. She finds a new home outside of the political mainstream. Now she is reading and discussing things such as *The Communist Manifesto* and *The Rich Get Richer and the Poor Get Prison* in a Zoom reading group, has bought tactical gear that she never considered doing before, and keeps 1,000 rounds of "green tip" military grade ammo for her newly acquired assault rifle. She regularly trains with her fellow members at one of their farms. She stands with her comrades in providing armed protection for BLM and peaceful Antifa protestors, but she has never raised a weapon or hand in that role. She is now "Redneck Revolt Rhonda," and she is truly dedicated to protecting this country from the rise of the Alt-Right, as well as protecting members of the working class and minorities from those who seek to harm them. She may even think that she has a future goal of seeing capitalism as it is presently configured undone and have a belief that violent means will be ultimately necessary.

Let us add that in the cases of both Ron and Rhonda, their friends and family are very concerned about the changes in each of them. They are disturbed by Ron's and Rhonda's new beliefs and ambitions as they are at odds with their own and strike them as at odds with Ron and Rhonda's former selves. Ron and Rhonda each became quite devoted to new their pursuits that, seemingly, rearranged their priorities in new ways, and these changes caused significant conflicts in their personal lives. They each had a marked increase in disputes with friends and loved ones that led to estrangement in some cases.

The "QAnon Ron" and "Redneck Revolt Rhonda" cases mimic reporting of peoples' stories in the likes of *Rolling Stone* (Dickson 2020; Morris 2021) as well as *Politico* (Jadeja 2021) of those who joined groups like QAnon and subsequently left. Many had been Sanders's supporters who were already primed to believe that behind the machinations of American politics and policy was a powerful economic elite—a cabal that has been pulling the strings. Their experience of the enthusiastic support for Sanders by Bernie Heads and his subsequent defeat in the primaries only seemed to reinforce this belief. Many were deflated by the hope that they had a candidate who appeared to be thriving but, ultimately, the apparent status quo was maintained by said elite by tampering with the primary process. Regardless of whether or not this was in fact true, it certainly made sense of their lived experience.

Political scientist Joseph Uscinsky (2021) has pointed out that many who are attracted to the most consuming conspiratorial worldviews are persons already prone to think that there are wider unseen machinations controlling what is happening in the world. It must be said that this need not be paranoid or delusional. There are indeed unexperienced factors at play in our social, economic, and political lives all of the time. There are forces in nature, the economy, in our own psychology about which we are not consciously aware. However, if one is more prone to seek understanding of things primarily in terms of unseen forces, then one is more likely to be primed for more disruptive conspiratorial worldviews. As for social media's role, Uscinsky (2021) goes on to argue that it is less about the algorithms pushing these views at us, than the algorithms revealing to us what we already desire to find. (Uscinsky's argument is also reported in Dickson 2021, Morris 2021, and Morrison 2019.) The algorithms are refined enough to feed us things that they have weighed from our internet behavior that we find attractive. If they were unsuccessful at predicting our attractions, the social media companies wouldn't compete in their market domain of selling advertising. The algorithms try to feed the desiring machine what it desires. It is part of what can make social media addictive. Uscinsky (2021) also notes that heading down these conspiratorial rabbit holes has less to do with political ideology than merely being prone to conspiratorial thinking—looking for hidden explanations of phenomena as trumping more direct or open explanations (see also Morris 2021). I wanted to acknowledge this possibility in my cases by showing that one could just as easily go from a Sanders supporter to a member of QAnon supporting Trump as to a member of a local chapter of the John Brown Gun Club preparing for the proletariat to rise up; thus, I created the divergent cases of "QAnon Ron" and "Redneck Revolt Rhonda." I also note that I built into these cases that neither Ron nor Rhonda had yet done anything criminal in order to hinder any bias that may arise from judging some clearly egregious behavior but instead keep a focus on that rearrangement of their beliefs, attitudes, and goals that make up their new worldviews. I want to focus on what we can or may do when with their envisioning personal projects that they see as making their lives meaningful and authentic and this causes conflict prior to any clear wrongdoing.

Veering away from having "QAnon Ron" and "Redneck Revolt Rhonda" engaging in any actual illegal behavior or doing harm helps us see that there is a problematic ethical dimension worth investigating prior to such things. People are often engaged in project-making life choices that impact those closest to them, but they have not yet done anything that a liberal, civil society would find "objectionable" in the pursuit of their projects. They have violated no one else's liberty or caused any direct, intentional harm. They may already be alienating friends and family and have given up on prior obligations that were tied to now abandoned goals, and so on, but they have not acted in any ways that should invoke any repercussions in a liberal society committed to value neutrality about individual good. They may have jettisoned activities they had loved for a long time or abandoned practices that were beneficial to them for new practices that appear to be riskier to themselves or others, but this is no basis for judgment or interference within liberal ethical and political traditions. I avoided having Ron or Rhonda engaging in harmful or illegal behavior to highlight that there are interesting questions about the value of personal projects, even ethical questions, before we even get to the question of wrongful actions that overstep the limits of protecting the liberty of others, and the point at which it apparently would make the cases ethically "easy." What I think experience shows and these cases raise is that, if Ron or Rhonda did come to act wrongfully, we have already missed serious opportunities for ethical engagement, because they or we have ignored thinking about the value of personal projects and what to do in cases of conflict with them. Here I am thinking about how we should engage people when their choosing a meaningful life project can cause personal and social disruption short of serious harm or illegal action, what we do about judgments of character in such times, and how we should deal with each other during such conflicts and, especially, when the outcome of any such projects are still a matter of resultant luck? Here I will take a cue from the stories of those who successfully left life projects that caused such early disagreements and contortions in personal lives. Sometimes these new personal projects led people to wrongful actions, but sometimes they got out before they did act in ways that would have brought a civil response. From those stories we can elicit an approach that addresses our set of questions in ways that is not a set of rules but a strategy of being with others.

COMPASSION AND INTERNAL REASONS

In the stories of those people who discovered and chose new projects around which to organize their lives and in which they found meaning, we discover that they often faced conflict with those closest to them. Their friends and family did not understand the sudden rearrangement of their concerns, goals, beliefs, and the actions that flowed from their new project that now animated their life with purpose and meaning. With social media and the internet providing ready access to so many new projects and perspectives, people are more likely to have friends and family considering or even choosing projects and perspectives that seem uncharacteristic to their history and exotic to the family or local culture. And when these perspectives seem fantastical and motivate actions that appear to be psychologically, economically, socially, epistemologically, or even legally harmful, tensions rise between caring intimates.

As microcommunities or novel worldviews spread, we can see families, communities, and even larger groups of the body politic fracture and become estranged from others with whom they were once close. The question becomes, what is the best way to handle people or even groups that have found novel worldviews that from another point of view appear misguided or even dangerous? This is especially a question of what may be done at a time prior to any illegal or immoral action being taken but where divisiveness is already felt between those who once had convivial social relations.

Psychologically and experientially, we already know that arguing and trying to get one's friend or loved one to capitulate is rarely successful. If someone has found a worldview to transform the meaning of their lives, arguing will rarely bring reconciliation or understanding. However, experience has also shown that when persons close to someone who has undergone a disruptive transformation are willing to meet them with empathetic listening that this can be constructive and mitigate deepening divisiveness. An empathetic listener, experience suggests, is someone who would note where they were in agreement, and often validate that they saw the other person's change of perspective and attitude as motivated by good intentions. However, this empathetic friend or loved one would also gently point out to their interlocutor where beliefs or actions taken were not consistent with their interlocutor's values or did not appear to be true. Finally, these empathetic listeners also allowed the person time to then come to their own conclusion rather than force them to admit defeat. Such friends or loved ones also had to demonstrate that they are open to being challenged with regard to their beliefs and actions as well. For lack of a better term, this seems like an approach of compassionate handling of those with whom we have divergent worldviews. This method is not at all foreign to those who work in therapeutic circles. It is a kind of empathic listening. This is to work with individuals' "internal reasons," as Williams (1981b, 101ff) may call it—such reasons can be shared between people or only held by the person who has found this new project.

Internal reasons, according to Williams (1981b) in his essay "Internal and External Reasons," are beliefs or attitudes that subjectively motivate a person to action, and these motives are often tied to their projects or worldviews. As a compassionate listener, one could identify in one's interlocutor their internal reasons or what motivates their beliefs, attitudes, or actions (101–6). For instance, in both the cases of "QAnon Ron" and "Redneck Revolt Rhonda," there is an underlying concern for those who are disempowered or have been marginalized, as well as a concern for the future of the United States as a nation. These may be motivations shared by a concerned loved one and a source for not alienating Ron or Rhonda, but it can also be a source when beliefs they voice or actions they take seem to conflict with those motivations. These internal reasons become values from which one can gently ask critical questions (and be asked critical questions in turn). If done in a nonconfrontational way, but as an invitation to consider their own beliefs, then it becomes a point for mutual dialogue across disparate points of view that may initially cause discomfort not from the vantage point of an attack, but from sources of mutual concern or even from just their own concerns. Granted, as an interlocutor, the compassionate listener should be willing to have their own beliefs and actions subjected to the same.

One advantage of this approach is that such an internal reasoning model of compassion gives hope of mitigating divisive relations and estrangement without the need for some set of transcendent moral principles or rules. One need not have some moral theory from on high to have a substantive critical discussion, because one can have a critical discussion within the person's very own set of values of beliefs (which may very likely include some values or beliefs that are shared). This process needs only the value commitments or internal reasons that are at play. Another advantage, when done well, is that it allows the individual to come to judge for themselves whether or not they are out of phase with their own commitments and gives them the freedom to change their mind. Finally, it is a means of approaching disagreement in a way that is between aggression and detachment, which holds hope of maintaining or reestablishing social connections. We know from real cases of individuals that this process of compassionate listening can successfully reduce divisiveness, and it can bring people to reassess potentially extreme attitudes and beliefs they hold. It will not always succeed, but it appears to have better results than direct argument. From the point of view of our ethical questions, this compassionate approach seems to hold promise of maintaining individuality while reducing interpersonal conflict and possibly increasing intersubjective understanding. However, it also requires that we work with the active values that are involved in people's projects, in what they take to be good and are their internal reasons. This seems to be promising at the individual level, but it may be more challenging at the macro-level of society. However, a collective version of such a process may hold some promise to avoid a dark Schmittian-like prediction where liberal, pluralistic societies internalize their own enemies and devour themselves from within (Schmitt 1976).

As noted, this model is inspired by the stories of friends and loved ones who hung in there with those persons who thought that QAnon offered a worldview and project which made things meaningful, and these individuals were compassionately listened to in the way outlined above. Subsequently, many came to see how what they believed and what they were doing and willing to do did not cohere as a meaningful project. We see similar stories with those who have exited other worldviews and projects that held deep meaning for them but which they ultimately left. They often had either a compassionate listener who had made this transition before or someone able to engage in the ways outlined above (Melton 2021; Pierre 2020). However, this method of successful compassionate dialogue, or internal reasoning, is not limited to successfully engaging those who had taken up QAnon as a meaningful life project. It is effective in bridging much conflict between those who disagree, and it is a method that does not rely on anyone having some insight into a "correct" perspective. As I said earlier, this is not a novel approach to interacting with others as it has long been used in counseling as a means to aid others to reflect on their own feelings, beliefs, values, and actions. However, it is a view that is not exactly value neutral nor is it entirely impartial. It utilizes internal reasons, motivating reasons, as values against which both parties are gauging what they will ultimately be willing to accept. How this process might look at a societal level, however, I will have to leave for another time. I would like to finish with two problems—one theoretical and the other practical.

MEANING, THE POSTMODERN CONDITION, AND SOCIAL MEDIA

I have generally treated individuals as entities that want to believe that their lives have meaning or value and that they have some control over this. Here, I use "meaning" as something akin to "having a purpose." Even if individuals aren't afforded such a luxury as the time to reflect on the goals of their life, it seems that when what they find important is challenged as being frivolous or repugnant, and so on, they often feel or display reactive emotions that expose the value they place on that thing or activity (and they feel or display positive reactive emotions when praised for those things they find important). In addition, their own sense of well-being rises and falls with how well that thing or activity is faring in the world (Frankfurt 1988, 260; Tillich 1958, 4–8). These experiences display what objects and activities they find meaningful to them. I also believe that the human desire for meaning or purpose, although it will obviously be influenced in many ways by culture and idiosyncratic historical details of a person's life, tends to be an individual's desire that their life has a purpose and that they have some agency in the success or failure in that endeavor. This is a very basic and general assumption I am making, and I am fully aware that this sounds quaint. This is a "humanist," "egocentric," and "Western" assumption, but a full explication of the view would take an entirely different paper.

Some thinkers may recoil from this "naïve," "antiquated" humanistic assumption. How can one believe in a voluntaristic self after postmodernism? My view is that there is still a trace of this humanistic ideal that remains even after the deconstruction of the self and even in the embrace of various post-humanist approaches to which I am thoroughly sympathetic. The idea of the humanistic, free-choosing self remains in some liberationist hope (however, limited that hope may be) that often runs through post-humanist accounts that allude to various ways in which such analyses of subjectivity are emancipatory (even if such an emancipation is brief and in need of constant vigilance since new reifications will only then constrain the self again). I am even willing to admit that this remains of a humanistic self may itself still be a vestige of our intellectual history and, in days to come, will be entirely erased but, today, it appears to still be with us. "QAnon Ron's" or "Redneck Revolt Rhonda's" conversions and internal reasons maintain an espousal of a liberating decision. They each committed to an individual purpose or project and act on behalf of them in order to give their lives meaning over which they have some sense of agency. Simply by virtue of the importance they place on wanting to want their commitments and to act on their behalf is evidence of that remaining humanism in our thought.

To keep things lean, the core assumption about people seeking meaning or living in ways that they believe to be engaged positively with their purpose(s) constitutes an important element of living well (even if people sometimes or even often engage in self-deception about how they are doing or even whether or not they would, in the end, be dedicated to their purpose). This is a claim about human experience that has been shared by a diverse set of thinkers in the European tradition to which, no matter how diffused now, we still have a thread of connection.

We have it in the American vernacular lineage from George Mason and Thomas Jefferson's declaration that each of us has a right to "liberty . . . and the pursuit of happiness." This rhetoric still has a strong hold on many. In the wider European context, existentialists, both theists and atheists alike, have held that in the face of a world that appears to be meaningless, we constitute or choose what our lives mean. An existentialist theme of the world not clearly providing an objective meaning for human existence, or showing us our purpose, goes back as far as St. Augustine's *Confessions*. To the idea that among competing visions of the world we must take a leap of faith, and in this we will ultimately find our purpose and meaning, Augustine was a pivotal figure. Paul Tillich (1958) argues that the meaning of "faith" is that which is of "ultimate concern" to us and having an object of faith constitutively orients us to how the world and our actions in it are meaningful to us (3–5). J. P. Sartre (1989) states in *Existentialism is a Humanism* that "man will only attain existence when he is what he purposes to be." In the absence of a God-given purpose, for Sartre, we are radically responsible for our own existence through making our own meaning. There are other thinkers from different philosophical lineages that also emphasize that we desire meaning and purpose and that it is personal and requires some agency. This voluntarism still has a stronghold through numerous sources in our culture. Harry Frankfurt (1988), in *The Importance of What We Care About*, explores the fact that having objects of concern or care are essential to having volition and having a life that has a sense of value. Albeit Frankfurt admits that while the discovery and hold objects or activities may have over us may not be entirely volitional, we do still have enough agency over their sway and our actions to see them as deeply personal and to see that we are responsible for our actions around what we do on their behalf (262–63). Similarly, Susan Wolf and John Koethe (2010), *The Meaning of Life (and Why It Matters)*, describe us as subjects that do not flourish without meaning, and that we do so when we combine a passion or love for something with an object that is, at least, understood to transcend that of the mere self-interest (8–10). Even those who play with Nietzsche's nihilism often have proposals about the positive creation of meaning that may come out in forms that still have a trace of a quasi-voluntaristic, creator-as-a-vector that sees possibilities in the multiplicities that emerge in the chaotic elements of destruction and assemblage that they envision (Deleuze and Guattari 1988, 24–25).

For much of the European tradition, the desire for purpose or meaning had been met by choosing among fairly homogeneous and widely shared "metanarratives," as Jean Francois Lyotard (1984) named them in *The Postmodern Condition* (xxiv). However, a characteristic of the last quarter of the twentieth and on into the twenty-first century, for a host of sociohistorical and intellectual reasons, was a crisis for the dominant metanarratives of European culture. Neither the story of legacy religion nor scientific enlightenment were holding positions of authority anymore. Lyotard (1984) and other postmodern thinkers saw opportunity and possibility in the demise of the standard metanarratives of European stories of progress, liberation, and ultimately salvation (whether it was through science or religious enlightenment). They saw possibilities of creativity, novelty, and new ways to undo hidden forms of subjugation. Others, such as Allan Bloom (1987) or Alasdair MacIntyre (2007), bemoaned the loss of core European metanarratives in different ways, as well as the dissolution of a unified community with a shared story and set of values. They saw impending chaos and the need for us to have a common story. Bloom (1987) and MacIntyre (2007) each tried to salvage this in a way of recouping or preserving the past—one through the preservation of the "Western" Canon and the other through a return to Aristotle and the need of finding a new Benedict of Nursia (I take it as a calling for something like the Rules of St. Benedict or some tradition of principled dogma). Whether for good or ill, I think the overall diagnosis of being in a postmodern condition and having lost shared narrative(s) is correct.

Jonathan Haidt (2022) nicely captures how the metanarratives of modernism that upheld strong democracies have been eroded by social media. Dominant metanarratives which we all shared or unified as a community, even broadly, no longer exist. Although Lyotard wrote *The Postmodern Condition* in the 1970s, Haidt (2022) argues that a true culmination of the condition is between 2011 and 2015 as social media siloed people into factions through desires-based targeted content that reinforced that people only follow their desires. In social media, according to Haidt (2022) anything that didn't fit their desires became deemed anything from boring to toxic, repugnant, evil, and so on. It was likely not the intent of social media entrepreneurs to undo a cohesive society (because frankly that usually isn't good for business). However, according to Haidt (2022), forty years after the fall of communism and thirty years after the advent of the internet and its commodification of peoples' time, eyes, and personal data, it seems to have successfully reversed *E Pluribus Unum*. Of course, it also made lots of cats available. Those of us in the developed world who had lost trust in the old metanarratives had a plethora of information at our fingertips and still do, but in social media that has been uniquely curated to our desires with the effect of siloing us with our closest like-minded individuals. Amidst all of this, I suggest there lingers, in "liking," "posting," "sharing," "ranting," and so on, and in expressing who we are, the trace or remnants of a desire to be a person with an expressed purpose (even if it's ultimately to be "internet famous"). We still desire an individual purpose to make our lives meaningful. There is still a trace of that old humanist ideal to which we aspire even in a postmodern, data- and image-saturated world. It may be nostalgia, but it still has a hold. It's just that now the projects through which we find meaning have become fractured, Balkanized, and multifarious.

Social media was launched as a tool for social connection between people. However, it was also a business. What could it sell without simply charging access to its users? It commodified users for their customers (their advertisers). According to social media app designers, they learned to build applications that utilize our own human psychology to get us to use their applications as often and as long as possible, and through that they can learn more from us and make their algorithms better in delivering advertising to specific users. However, they also are able to learn about us in ways that will keep us on their apps more often and longer by feeding us content which their algorithms predict we desire, and we might find meaningful. If successful, they can charge more for advertising. The fact that one-third of the earth's population now uses some social media platform (less than twenty years after their introduction) means that this is a huge source of potential advertising income (Ortiz-Ospina 2019). This is not a criticism, but a simple explanation of their business model and their success in achieving what they do. For my interests here, the issue is that in a postmodern world the realm of the internet and social media (which are completely fluid), coupled with peoples' desires to have meaningful or purposeful lives that remains in the cultural milieu, means that more and more people will likely discover meaningful projects via social media connections. And the array of content or connections offered, even if limited by an algorithm to those that are related to those desires expressed by the users, can still offer content or connections which ultimately may place users in discord with their past self and with others. And this is part of the postmodern condition. It may be that compassionately listening to others is what is needed to break beyond the silos, but first we may have to step away from our computers and put our phones down more often and try to engage with friends, family, and people in our communities with whom we have strained relations.

COMPASSION AND THE LIMITS OF TOLERANCE

A concern that could be raised about the approach suggested here is twofold. On the one hand, it may be thought that it is too invasive of people's liberty. It asks us to delve into the beliefs and values that make up others' life projects, into their individual ideas about the good life, when their plans and actions create conflict for us. This appears to invite meddling and conflict, and it also appears to abandon the impartiality that we so value in a liberal, pluralistic society. On the other hand, it appears that it may not be liberty-conducive enough. Since this view appears to require more humility and restraint, more tolerance, on the part of the compassionate listener than it does on the part of their interlocutor, it denies the compassionate listener the freedom to set their own limits to what is tolerable. Here I want to suggest that each of these worries is a genuine practical concern, but the process has promise to keep each interlocutor's liberty as unhindered as materially allowable.

We are motivated by internal reasons. Even if these motivating reasons are acquired from elsewhere, if we want to want them, then they are ours. These reasons reflect objects we care about, at least those most compelling to us; so, we see our own well-being rising and falling with the welfare of those objects. Thus, to really get at the source of where we are in tension with another person over different life plans, we must listen to what motivates them. Simply adhering to some public standards of noninterference is completely compatible with a world of isolated individuals, lonely and non-connected. We would have a world of non-harm, but no aid and no connection. But, as Kant so rightly points out, we need others to engage in our plans—to seek our own good. Thus, it is best if we understand what each other is seeking and why, especially among intimates. Exploring each other's ideas of the good life, what makes life meaningful, and what is important are inescapable, if we are to live together. This can be done well or badly.

The process outlined above—one that has been practiced regularly by many in religious and therapeutic circles—has a track record for first eliciting people to share their own beliefs, values, and so on, in a nonhostile environment. It invites people to share their ideas of what makes their life meaningful or what they care about. In this way, it is intrusive, but it is an invitation which they can decline. It is also a process that never tells the person what they should learn from the discussions but allows them to discover new ideas for themselves. In this way, it is thus not excessively intrusive. If the person refuses the invitation or simply remains recalcitrant to reflecting on their own internal reasons, then the compassionate listener has a choice to make about what they are willing to live with. They have the same freedom to explore what limits of behavior or values they are willing to live with and to tolerate. The compassionate listener has projects with values attached as well. The view does not require the compassionate listener to capitulate and accept the values of the other person. In the same way that they are asking their interlocutor to expose and potentially reflect on their internal reasons and the actions that flow from them, so should the compassionate listener. If they do not do so, they risk tolerating the intolerable and being a doormat to the other person's values and project. This is not easy for either member of the process, especially as friends or loved ones, or if members have strong attachments to opposing projects involved. It does take a special type of motivation, a decision to want to attempt to see the maintenance of fellowship of some value, and it takes abilities to maintain a level of humility, composure, and patience at least by the compassionate listener to see if the process will succeed. It will also take some wisdom to understand one's limits and when it might be time to end the process, if success in maintaining or achieving good fellowship looks bleak (because it will not be successful in all cases). The hope I extend here is that some model of compassionate listening can be an effective resource for salvaging relations between people when ideals of good living and personal projects give rise to deeply-felt, interpersonal struggles.

CONCLUSION

When COVID-19 suddenly shut off the world, many more people were more often reaching out through social media. Social media has been technologically engineered quickly to more masterfully target things of interest to users so as to keep their eyes longer and more often in their apps; thus, social media harnessed their desires so as to keep advertising dollars flowing. At this time, there is a remaining desire for an authentic and meaningful existence that is our own (no matter how tattered the late metanarratives have become). The internet opened the possibility of myriad novel narratives from which we can choose, and the algorithms in social media are now tailoring connections to some of those we may find fit our demonstrated desires. Some of us may latch onto new projects with narratives that put us in conflict with our past selves and with those close to us and to our wider communities. Some of those may be potentially harmful and this is concerning, especially with the present state of fractured communities where dialogue with others may be seen as itself lacking commitment to a cause. A simple state of "let others be and don't interfere" may be long past, and we need to be willing to discuss what others find worth living for. We have to pierce this liberal veil of neutrality while granting as much liberty as possible to all involved. The hope outlined here is that something akin to compassionate listening provides a model (although I am sure it is not the only model). Friends, family, or community members of "QAnon Ron" or "Redneck Revolt Rhonda" can invite them to share their reasons and make connection with others to lace a fractured society back together—at least in ways that aren't seemingly motivated by constant threat of harm. Like many a Gen Xer, I am prone to cynicism generally. However, there is plenty of evidence that this model has worked well among individuals. Thus, I here offer hope. We have actually been doing it for centuries, and it has become a hallmark method of clinical psychology. The hope is that we can do this between individuals with the aim of rebuilding communities that have seemingly fractured in late postmodernity. I just hope that I am not whistling in the dark, dim light of a mobile screen.

REFERENCES

Bloom, Allan. 1987. *The Closing of the American Mind: How Higher Education Has Failed Democracy and Impoverished the Souls of Today's Students*. New York: Simon and Schuster.

CBS Miami. 2020. "COVID Pandemic Has Led to Spike in Americans Searching for Family They Never Knew." *CBS Miami*. Last Modified October 12. https://miami.cbslocal.com/2020/10/12/covid-pandemic-americans-ancestry-search.

Collins, Ben. "Transcript: Into the Rise of QAnon during the Pandemic." Interviewed by Trymaine Lee. *Into America*, MSNBC, August 20. www.msnbc.com/podcast/transcript-rise-qanon-during-pandemic-n1237524.

Deleuze, Gilles, and Félix Guattari. 1988. *A Thousand Plateaus: Capitalism and Schizophrenia*. London: Athlone.

De-Wit, Lee, Sander Van Der Linden, and Cameron Brick. 2019. "Are Social Media Driving Political Polarization?" *Greater Good*. Last Modified January 6. https://greatergood.berkeley.edu/article/item/is_social_media_driving_political_polarization.

Dickson, E .J. 2020. "Former QAnon Followers Explain What Drew Them In—and Got Them Out." *Rolling Stone*. Last Modified September 23. www.rollingstone.com/culture/culture-features/ex-qanon-followers-cult-conspiracy-theory-pizza-gate-1064076.

Frankfurt, Harry G. 1988. *The Importance of What We Care About: Philosophical Essays*. Cambridge: Cambridge University Press.

Haidt, Jonathan. 2022. "Why the Past 10 Years of American Life Have Been Uniquely Stupid." *The Atlantic*. Last Modified April 11. www.theatlantic.com/magazine/archive/2022/05/social-media-democracy-trust-babel/629369.

Jadeja, Jitarth. "I Left QAnon in 2019. But I'm Still Not Free." Interviewed by Anastasiia Carrier, *Politico,* December 11. www.politico.com/news/magazine/2021/12/11/q-anon-movement-former-believer-523972.

Kantar. 2020. "COVID-19 Barometer: Consumer Attitudes, Media Habits and Expectations." Last Modified April 3. www.kantar.com/Inspiration/Coronavirus/COVID-19-Barometer-Consumer-attitudes-media-habits-and-expectations.

Lyotard, Jean-François, Bennington, Geoffrey, and Brian Massumi. 1984. *The Postmodern Condition: A Report on Knowledge*. Minneapolis, MN: University of Minnesota Press.

MacIntyre, Alasdair C. 2007. *After Virtue: A Study in Moral Theory*. 3rd ed. Notre Dame, IN: University of Notre Dame Press.

Marx, Karl, Friedrich Engels, A. J. P. Taylor, and Samuel Moore. 1985. *The Communist Manifesto*. London: Penguin Books.

McClain, Colleen, Emily A. Vogels, Andrew Perrin, Stella Sechopoulos, and Lee Rainie. 2021. "The Internet and the Pandemic." Last Modified September 1. www.pewresearch.org/internet/2021/09/01/the-internet-and-the-pandemic.

Melton, Marissa. 2021. "As QAnon Strains Relationships, Loved Ones Try to Show a Way Out." *Voice of America*. Last Modified July 18. www.voanews.com/a/usa_qanon-strains-relationships-loved-ones-try-show-way-out/6208393.html.

Morris, Alex. 2021. "It's Not Q. It's You." *Rolling Stone*. Last Modified October 15. www.rollingstone.com/culture/culture-features/qanon-expert-joesph-uscinski-1242636.

Morrison, Patt. "Column: How Much Are Conspiracy Theories Really Shaping American Life?" *Los Angeles Times*. Last Modified August 13. www.latimes.com/opinion/story/2019-08-13/patt-morrison-joseph-uscinski-white-supremacy-conspiracy.

Ortiz-Ospina, Estaban. 2019 "The Rise of Social Media." Last Modified September 18. https://ourworldindata.org/rise-of-social-media.

Pierre, Joe. 2020. "4 Keys to Help Someone Climb Out of the QAnon Rabbit Hole." *Psychology Today*. Last Modified September 1. www.psychologytoday.com/us/blog/psych-unseen/202009/4-keys-help-someone-climb-out-the-qanon-rabbit-hole.

Reiman, Jeffrey H. 2007. *The Rich Get Richer and the Poor Get Prison: Ideology, Class, and Criminal Justice*. 8th ed. Boston, MA: Pearson/Allyn & Bacon.

Sartre, Jean-Paul. 1989. "Existentialism Is a Humanism." From *Existentialism from Dostoyevsky to Sartre*, edited by Walter Kaufman. Last Modified February 2005. www.marxists.org/reference/archive/sartre/works/exist/sartre.htm.

Schmitt, Carl. 1976. *The Concept of the Political*. New Brunswick, NJ: Rutgers University Press.

Smart, John Jamieson Carswell, and Bernard Arthur Owen Williams. 1973. *Utilitarianism: For and Against*. Cambridge: Cambridge University Press.

Tillich, Paul. 1958. *Dynamics of Faith*. New York: Harper.

Uscinski, Joseph. 2021. "Clear Thinking about Conspiracy Theories in Troubled Times." *Skeptical Inquirer* 45, no. 1 (January/February). https://skepticalinquirer.org/2021/01/clear-thinking-about-conspiracy-theories-in-troubled-times.

Williams, Bernard Arthur Owen. 1981a. *Moral Luck: Philosophical Papers, 1973–1980*. Cambridge: Cambridge University Press.

———. 1981b. "Internal and External Reasons." In *Moral Luck: Philosophical Papers*, 101–13. Cambridge: Cambridge University Press.

———. 1981c. Moral Luck." In *Moral Luck: Philosophical Papers*, 20–39. Cambridge: Cambridge University Press.

———. 1981d. "Persons, Character and Morality." In *Moral Luck: Philosophical Papers*, 1–19. Cambridge: Cambridge University Press.

———. 1985. *Ethics and the Limits of Philosophy*. Cambridge: Harvard University Press.

Wolf, Susan R., and John Koethe. 2010. *Meaning in Life and Why It Matters*. Princeton, NJ: Princeton University Press.

Appendix
Chapter 3 Survey Instrument

The survey instrument below is used in chapter 3, "Social Media, COVID-19, Misinformation, and Ethics: A Descriptive Study of American Adults' Perceptions," by Tammy Swenson-Lepper and Heidi J. Hanson. (*Note: Please request permission to use this survey in your own research from the first author, Tammy Swenson-Lepper: tswensonlepper@winona.edu.*)

SOCIAL MEDIA, COVID-19, AND ETHICS SURVEY

Throughout this survey, we refer to social media. When we refer to social media, we mean TikTok, Instagram, Snapchat, Facebook, and Twitter. We will also occasionally refer to YouTube as a social media platform, depending on the question.

The earliest questions in the survey will take the longest. Please hang in there and share your opinions!

1. I have used social media for:
   a) A few months
   b) A year
   c) Two to three years
   d) Four to five years
   e) Six to seven years
   f) Eight years to nine years
   g) Ten years or more
2. Please check all of the social media apps you use regularly.
   a) Facebook

b) Instagram
   c) Snapchat
   d) TikTok
   e) Twitter
3. I check Facebook: (appears only if Facebook is checked in Q3)
   a) Several times an hour
   b) Several times a day
   c) At least once a day
   d) Once a week
   e) Rarely
4. I check Instagram:
   a) Several times an hour
   b) Several times a day
   c) At least once a day
   d) Once a week
   e) Rarely
5. I use Snapchat:
   a) Several times an hour
   b) Several times a day
   c) At least once a day
   d) Once a week
   e) Rarely
6. I check TikTok:
   a) Several times an hour
   b) Several times a day
   c) At least once a day
   d) Once a week
   e) Rarely
7. I check Twitter:
   a) Several times an hour
   b) Several times a day
   c) At least once a day
   d) Once a week
   e) Rarely
8. How would you define misinformation? Can you provide an example of misinformation that you've seen? _____
9. Do you think there should be a consequence for social media companies for sharing misinformation about COVID-19, the vaccine for COVID-19, and masks on social media? Why or why not? What should the punishment be, if any? _____
10. Do you think there should be a consequence for individuals for sharing misinformation about COVID-19, the vaccine for COVID-19, and masks

on social media? Why or why not? What should the punishment be, if any? _____
11. What is the biggest ethical issue you notice related to COVID-19, the vaccine for COVID-19, and masks on social media? Why do you think that is an ethical issue? _____
12. What are the most *unethical* ways that you've seen social media used in relationship to COVID-19, the vaccine for COVID-19, and masks on social media? Can you give examples? _____
13. How have your views of ethical issues related to COVID-19, the vaccine for COVID-19, and masks on social media changed from when the pandemic first started? _____
14. Please answer the following questions about your experiences with social media honestly. (Rate from Strongly Disagree to Strongly Agree.)
    a) I have believed something about COVID-19 on social media that I believed to be true, but later learned was false.
    b) I have believed something about the vaccines for COVID-19 on social media that I believed to be true, but later learned was false.
    c) I have believed something about masking as a way to prevent the spread of COVID-19 on social media that I believed to be true, but later learned was false.
    d) I thoroughly check the sources of social media posts about COVID-19, the vaccine for COVID-19, and masking.
    e) Negative experiences online related to COVID-19, the COVID-19 vaccine, and masking have decreased my use of social media.
    f) I have a more positive opinion of social media than I did three years ago.
15. Please answer the following questions about your experiences with social media honestly. (Rate from Strongly Disagree to Strongly Agree.)
    a) I have unintentionally shared fake news or misinformation about the COVID-19 virus on social media.
    b) I have unintentionally shared fake news or misinformation about the COVID-19 vaccine on social media.
    c) I have unintentionally shared fake news or misinformation about the value of masking for preventing COVID-19 on social media.
    d) My friends or family have shared fake news or misinformation about the COVID-19 virus on social media.
    e) My friends or family have shared fake news or misinformation about the COVID-19 vaccines on social media.
    f) My friends or family have shared fake news or misinformation about the value of masking for preventing COVID-19 on social media.
16. Please answer the following questions about your experiences with social media honestly. (Rate from Strongly Disagree to Strongly Agree.)

a) When I've stated my opinions about COVID-19 on social media, I've been verbally attacked by other social media users in the comments.
b) When my friends have stated their opinions about COVID-19 on social media, I've seen them be verbally attacked in the comments.
c) When I've stated my opinions about mask-wearing in relationship to COVID-19 on social media, I've been verbally attacked by other social media users in the comments.
d) When my friends have stated their opinions about mask-wearing in relationship to COVID-19 on social media, I've seen them be verbally attacked in the comments.
e) When I've stated my opinions about vaccinations in relationship to COVID-19 on social media, I've been verbally attacked by other social media users in the comments.
f) When my friends have stated their opinions about vaccinations in relationship to COVID-19 on social media, I've seen them be verbally attacked in the comments.
g) I have refrained from sharing information related to COVID-19, masking, or vaccines on social media in fear of a negative response.

17. Please answer the following questions about your experiences with social media and COVID-19 honestly. (Rate from Strongly Disagree to Strongly Agree.)
    a) If a social media post related to COVID-19 provides sources, I research the sources to ensure their validity.
    b) I question shared information on social media regarding COVID-19 rather than immediately taking it at face value.
    c) I have shared information related to COVID-19 on social media because a lot of my peers or family members had also shared the same information.
    d) I have shared information related to COVID-19 I don't 100 percent agree with because a lot of my peers or family members had also shared the same information.
    e) When information on social media related to COVID-19 does not align with my previous views about COVID-19, I assume it is unimportant or incorrect.
    f) I am more likely to reshare or repost information related to COVID-19 on social media if it is presented in an aesthetically pleasing way.
    g) My posting or sharing of information regarding COVID-19 on social media has led to issues and/or arguments taking place with my family or friends.

h) I have had negative feelings regarding a social media post related to COVID-19 information posted by my friends or family members.
18. In my experience, misinformation and fake news about COVID-19, the vaccine against COVID-10, and masking is worst on which platforms? (Drag the name of the platforms in order from worst to best, with number 1 being the social media platform that you think is the greatest source for misinformation and fake news.)
   a) Facebook
   b) Instagram
   c) Snapchat
   d) TikTok
   e) Twitter
   f) YouTube
19. How closely have you followed news: (Rate from Very Closely to Not at All Closely.)
   a) About the COVID-19 virus?
   b) About the COVID-19 vaccine?
   c) About the use of masks to prevent the spread of COVID-19?
20. I primarily get my news about COVID-19, COVID-19 vaccines, and masking from: (Rate from Never to Always.)
   a) National evening news (such as ABC World News, CBS Evening News, or NBC Nightly News)
   b) Cable television news, such as CNN, Fox, or MSNBC
   c) Local television news
   d) Print newspapers
   e) Online newspapers or online news apps.
   f) Social Media, such as Twitter, Facebook, Instagram, Snapchat, or TikTok
   g) YouTube
21. What is your primary source of news? Please name it here.
   _____
22. Generally speaking, do you usually think of yourself as a Democrat, an Independent, a Republican, or something else?
   a) Democrat
   b) Independent
   c) Republican
   d) Other _____
23. If you think of yourself as a Democrat, how would you label yourself?
   a) Progressive Democrat
   b) Moderate Democrat
   c) Conservative Democrat
24. If you think of yourself as an Independent, how would you label yourself?

a) More similar to Republicans than Democrats
b) More similar to Democrats than Republicans
c) Equally similar to Republicans and Democrats
25. If you think of yourself as a Republican, how would you label yourself?
    a) Libertarian Republican
    b) Moderate Republican
    c) Conservative Republican
26. If you don't consider yourself a Democrat, Independent, or Republican, how would you label yourself politically? _____
27. I am
    a) a college or university student
    b) not a college or university student
28. I am a
    a) first-year student
    b) sophomore
    c) junior
    d) senior
    e) MA student
    f) PhD student
29. My highest level of education is:
    a) Some high school
    b) High school graduate, diploma, or the equivalent (e.g., GED)
    c) Some college credits, no degree
    d) Trade/technical/vocational training
    e) Associate's degree
    f) Bachelor's degree
    g) Master's degree
    h) Professional degree
    i) Doctoral degree
30. How old are you? (Please use a number, like 18 or 54.)
31. I am
    a) Female
    b) Male
    c) Transgender female
    d) Transgender male
    e) Gender variant/non-conforming
    f) Not listed _____
    g) Prefer not to answer
32. Race: Check as many boxes as you believe are appropriate to describe yourself.
    a) White
    b) Hispanic or Latino

c) Black or African American
d) American Indian, Native American, or Alaska Native
e) Asian
f) Native Hawaiian or Pacific Islander
g) Other
h) Prefer not to disclose

Index

bias, 136; confirmation, 58, 60; negativity, 58; source, 58
Bildung, 87
black-boxing/black-boxed, 13, 15, 18
bots (animated social media accounts), 15, 116–18

Clubhouse, 102
CNN, 41
compassionate listening, 4, 138–39, 143–45
connecting well, 10–11, 21
conservatives, 38, 40, 48, 53, 58, 64, 71, 119
conspiracy theories, 1, 3, 32–33, 36–37, 39, 41–43, 47, 53, 55–56, 58–59, 102, 115–17, 128; conspiracist narratives, 55
convergence culture, 33–34
COVID-19, 1–5, 10–11, 13–14, 18–20, 22–26, 31–34, 36–37, 39–41, 43–47, 49–50, 53–75, 85–91, 93–97, 99, 103–4, 109–21, 126, 134, 145; hoax/hoaxes, 38, 41, 53, 70, 134; lockdowns, 1, 4, 36–37, 39–40, 86, 88, 90–95, 97–100, 103, 111, 126–27; masking/mask-wearing, 4, 31, 40–41, 48–49, 54, 63–72, 74–76, 86, 89, 92, 103, 110–12, 115–20; vaccines/vaccinations, 11–12, 14, 24, 31, 36, 39, 45–47, 49, 53–55, 57, 63–73, 75–76, 86, 113, 116–17, 121, 134; virus, 1, 36–39, 41, 43–44, 53, 55, 58, 63–65, 67, 69–73, 75, 85–86, 96, 109, 113, 121

democrats, 38, 60, 64, 70–71, 111–13, 115–19, 134
dialogue, 9, 11–14, 18–27, 138–39, 145
digital repression, 15
directionality, 14, 16–20; bottom-up, 2–3, 9, 14, 16–17, 19–20, 23, 26–27; top-down, 2–3, 9, 14, 16–23, 25–26
disinformation, 1–2, 4–5, 10, 22, 55, 57, 60, 121
distanciation, 95
divisiveness, 129, 137, 139
Douyin, 100

emotivism, 90
epistemic responsibility, 9–10, 14–15, 19, 23, 26; connecting well, 10–11, 21; knowing well/know well, 9–13, 15–16, 18–21, 26–27
ethicality of social media posts, 2, 54, 63
expediency, 9, 11–14, 18–21, 23–24, 26–27

extremism/extremists, 55

Facebook, 37, 41, 43–44, 54–55, 59–61, 65–67, 70, 74, 91, 95, 100–102; Messenger, 91, 100
fake news, 12, 17, 38–39, 53–65, 70–72, 75
fandom, 34; anti-fandom, 33, 35, 44, 47
Fauci, Anthony, 41, 43–44, 48, 117–18
Freedom Convoy, 31
freedom of expression, 16, 21, 25
freedom of speech, 3, 9, 13, 16, 55, 63, 67–68, 75

Gates, Bill, 36, 39, 41–44, 47–48
Goodreads, 102
Google, 37, 41
Grand Old Party (GOP), 38, 118
group meaning making, 32

Hanks, Chet, 45, 48

infodemic, 9–14, 17–20, 22, 26–27, 71, 103
Instagram, 43, 45, 54, 67, 74, 91, 100, 102, 125
internal reasons, 137–40, 144
intersubjective understanding, 139

John Brown Gun Club, 134, 136

Kakao, 100

leisure, 1–2, 4, 85, 87–91, 93–100, 103–4
Liberalism, European, 4, 128–29
liberals, 58, 64
luck: moral, 4, 130–31; resultant, 131–32, 137

meaningful lives, 2, 128–29, 132
mental health, 56, 96–97, 100, 103–4; anxiety, 56, 96, 99–100, 126; depression, 100, 126; isolation/loneliness, 1, 4, 12, 36, 49, 99–101, 126, 144

metanarrative, 33–34, 37, 46, 142, 145
misinformation, 1–5, 9–27, 32–33, 43, 49–50, 53–57, 60, 62–67, 69–76, 74–76, 102, 121, 126

narcissism, 90
NBC, 41
news: apps, 54; coverage, 86; online, 54; social media and, 1–3, 33–36, 54–63, 99–100, 110
NextDoor, 102

online aggression, 11, 16, 21, 27
open-source, 13
Owens, Candace, 40

parental rights, 3, 39, 47–48
Peloton, 101
phenomenological rendering, 129
phenomenology, 131
Pinterest, 91, 100
plandemic, 3, 32–33, 36–37, 39, 41–46, 48–49
polarization, 3–5, 57–58, 110–11, 113, 120–21
private sector, 12, 127
public neutrality, 130

QAnon, 42, 49, 125, 128, 134–36, 138–40, 145
Quora, 100

Reddit, 3, 10, 20–26, 100
Redneck Revolt, 134–36, 138, 140, 145
religion, 68–70, 125, 142
Republicans, 60, 64, 71, 111–12, 115–20
rules of censure, 14–17, 19–20, 23–24

Sanders, Bernie, 132–33, 135–36
scamdemic, 3, 32–33, 36–43, 46, 48–49
Sina Weibo, 100
Snapchat, 54, 74, 91, 100, 102
Social+, 102
social distancing, 23, 92–93

social media platforms, 1–3, 9–17, 19–20, 26, 41, 43, 47, 54, 56–57, 65–67, 74, 89, 91, 95, 99–102, 113, 127, 143
social web, 9, 11, 15, 19, 27
spreadable media, 33–34, 43

Telegram, 100
third-person effect, 3, 4, 54, 59–61, 64, 71–73, 75
TikTok, 74, 91, 100–103
tourism, online, 4, 94
transparency, 14–15, 17–20, 25, 27, 50
Trump, Donald J., 2, 37–39, 41, 55, 69–71, 75, 118–21, 134, 136
Trump Jr., Donald, 45, 47
Twitter, 2–4, 10, 18, 20, 24–27, 32, 36–38, 40, 42–43, 45–46, 57, 65, 74, 100–102, 109–10, 113–14, 119–21

US Centers for Disease Control (CDC), 4, 13, 22–24, 40, 43–44, 46, 48, 86, 92, 114–20
US National Institutes of Health (NIH), 39

value neutrality, 129, 136
Venmo, 102

Wesbury, Brian, 40
WhatsApp, 74, 99–101
World Health Organization, 10, 22–24, 38, 41, 46, 86, 92

xenophobia, 56–57

YouTube, 3, 10, 22–26, 37, 42, 53–54, 59, 65, 74, 91, 100, 134

About the Contributors

Berrin A. Beasley is a professor in the School of Communication at the University of North Florida whose research focuses on social media ethics, gender stereotypes in the media, and journalism history. She's a former newspaper reporter and editor in Florida and New Mexico and coeditor of *Social Media Ethics: The Value of Truth*, which received a *Choice* award for outstanding academic book, and *Social Media and Living Well*. She's had numerous book chapters published on media ethics, and her research has been published in *Mass Communication and Society*, the *Newspaper Research Journal*, the *Journal of Radio Studies*, *Journalism Studies*, the *European Journal of Communication*, and *Electronic Media*, among other journals.

Miles C. Coleman is an assistant professor of communication studies at Rowan University. He studies constraints and affordances of computational media for productive engagements with science denialism on the internet. His research appears in such journals as *Human-Machine Communication*, *Philosophy & Rhetoric*, *Review of Communication*, *First Monday*, the *Journal of Media Ethics*, the *Journal of Aesthetics & Culture*, and the *Western Journal of Communication*, among others.

Mitchell R. Haney is an associate professor of philosophy and codirector of the Florida Blue Center for Ethics at the University of North Florida. He is the coeditor of *Social Media Ethics: The Value of Truth* and *Social Media and Living Well*.

Heidi J. Hanson is an undergraduate student at Winona State University and is majoring in Communication Arts and Literature-Teaching in order to be a high school English or communications teacher. She has served as a features writer for *The Winonan* (the Winona State University student newspaper), was a nominee for the Rising Star Award (for talented first-year students), and served as a WSU ambassador, giving tours of campus to prospective students. She enjoys reading, volunteers often, and looks forward to being a resident assistant on the WSU campus and features reporter for *The Winonan* in the upcoming years.

Annette M. Holba is a professor of rhetoric at Plymouth State University. Her scholarship focuses on the philosophy of communication, communication ethics, and philosophical leisure. She has published twelve books, over forty articles, eleven book chapters, and seven encyclopedic entries and has delivered over 100 scholarly presentations. Dr. Holba won the Everett Lee Hunt Book Award in the communication discipline (2013) for her coauthored book *An Overture to Philosophy of Communication: The Carrier of Meaning*, and again in 2022 for her book *Philosophy of Communication Inquiry: In Introduction*. Other recent awards include the following: ECA Journal Article of the Year (2015), NCA Article of the Year (2015), the Julia T. Wood Teacher Scholar Award (2021), and ECA Research Fellow (2021). Dr. Holba is past editor for *Qualitative Research Reports in Communication,* and she was just named the next editor for the *Journal of Dialogic Ethics*: *Interfaith and Interhuman Perspectives.*

Linda Howell is director of the writing program and center and a senior instructor at the University of North Florida. Her research focuses on fandom studies, composition, rhetoric, and new media.

Tammy Swenson-Lepper (PhD, University of Minnesota) is a professor and internship director in the Communication Studies Department at Winona State University. Her research interests include communication ethics, ethical sensitivity, pedagogy and communication ethics, organizational communication, and service learning. She is a former chair of the Communication Ethics Division of the National Communication Association. Her most recent publications include "Cyberbullies, Trolls, and Stalkers: Students' Perceptions of Ethical Issues in Social Media," in the *Journal of Media Ethics* (2019), and *Communication Ethics: Activities for Critical Thinking and Reflection* (Kendall Hunt, 2021), for which she wrote a chapter on communication ethics in social media.

Pamela A. Zeiser is a professor of political science at the University of North Florida in Jacksonville. She is the author of *Global Studies Research*, a textbook on interdiciplinary research methods. Her other publications are on the topics of social media, global health, U.S. foreign policy, pedagogy, and civic education. She has taught interdisciplinary international studies courses such as Global Issues in Contemporary Politics and Capstone Seminar: International Studies. In the discipline of political science, she offers a broad range of international relations and comparative politics courses, including International Law and Organization, Politics and Society in Britain and Ireland, and Global Health Politics. Her research has been published in the *Journal of Political Science Education*, *PS: Political Science and Politics*, *National Civic Review*, and *Women's Studies: An Interdisciplinary Journal*.

www.ingramcontent.com/pod-product-compliance
Lightning Source LLC
Chambersburg PA
CBHW020124010526
44115CB00008B/963